MW01251654

Journey to a New You

12 Habits to a Happy and Successful Life

Journey to a New You

12 Habits to a Happy and Successful Life

Cora Cristobal

ISBN-13: 978-1530575121

PUBLISHED BY:
10-10-10 PUBLISHING
MARKHAM, ON
CANADA

CONTENTS

Journey to a New You

12 Habits to a Happy and Successful Life

DEDICATION

This book is dedicated **to all the readers** in pursuit of success and happiness;

May this book help or motivate you towards it.

To my parents **Santos** and **Patrocinio**, who have been gone;
For giving me life and love.

To my children, **Laura, Rose, JR** and **Dino**;
To **Fidelino Tinapay**;
We built a family.

To my brothers **During, Inso, Perpe** who have departed;
To **Larry**, my younger brother, my only brother now alive;
For their protection and loving care.

To my sisters **Tessie, Nedy** and **Aida**;
For sharing with me their values of hard work, piety and sacrifice;
That I am proud of and emulate.

To my grandson **Leon Kasyanov**;
That he may start acquiring the right habits;
To grow up happily and successfully.

FOREWORD

Do you want to be happy and successful? Is this just an elusive dream or wishful thinking?

Cora Cristobal, a successful accountant, real estate investor, realtor, and now a coach and author, shares with you her secret; how she made it, through hard work and healthy habits.

This book about the 12 habits to a happy and successful life is very motivational and inspiring. It is written in simple language, yet the messages are powerful, and will teach you how to acquire, develop or change a habit towards success and happiness. After many years of personal struggles, successes and failures in both her personal life and career, Cora has compiled the top 12 habits that will ensure you will never be simply chasing your dreams.

This book covers habits concerning health, education, attitude, goal-setting, discipline and control, finances, relationships, gratitude and affirmations and self-improvements.

You will surely enjoy this marvelous book, as you learn that the pursuit to happiness and success is simple and easy. Enjoy!

Raymond Aaron
NY Times Bestselling Author

INTRODUCTION

" I am what I am today
because of the choices I made yesterday"
Stephen Covey

As it is said, we are all creatures of habits. And we all know what habits are. This is a routine of behavior that we do regularly and automatically without thinking first before doing it. This is acquired through previous repetition. Old habits are hard to break and new habits are not easy to form because the behavioral patterns are already imprinted in our brains. However, it is possible to form new habits by repetition. According to studies, the average time to develop a habit is 66 days.

We all continuously chase happiness. The thing is many of us are finding happiness that is temporary. Think of when you bought your house or your car, or when you travelled to a favorite destination, or when you were promoted in your job.

Good habits are self-maintaining and self-enhancing, and can lead to a happy, successful and productive life. I have noticed myself building permanent habits from when I was young and developing different habits from different stages of my life. I have also noticed that I have broken some habits, for one reason or another. And to my surprise, even at this time and at my age, I am still acquiring new habits just because I have goals to fulfill or desires to attain. So, I thought, habits must then be the anchor, or foundation leading to happiness or success. So, habits are very powerful! Because, to be happy or successful, we have to do something that will make us happy and successful. And from what I can see, the simple secret to success and happiness may be one's habits. Habits are the very foundations of our actions, impulses and decision making.

So, I analyzed my own life's successes and failures, my observations, my readings and interactions and decided to put them all together in this book. I hope you will find this useful and beneficial.

So, let us go down memory lane… What habits have I acquired and why did I acquire them? And what have they done to me? Have they brought me happiness, or sorrow? Have they caused me to have success, or failure ?

Over the years, from my childhood, to my adulthood, I have seen many people in different situations. People who have are happy and not so happy. People who are successful and not so successful. Many theories and articles have been written. In my own life, at this point in time, I have been intrigued as to why we are in different situations, and why success and happiness do not come at the same rate and phase for different people. I am not a psychologist to be able to explain this. I am writing this to share my own personal experiences, and what I have learned from the more successful and happier people.

In the BOLD (Business Objective, A Life By Design) by Dianne Kokoszka of Keller Williams Real Estate Coaching workshop that I attended when I started my real estate career in Canada in the early 2008, I have learned that you can actually create your real estate sales income by design and not by default. Not by chance, but by conscious, determined effort. Indeed, Dianne Kokoszka's BOLD techniques propelled her million dollar real estate career and she was branded the *"queen of real estate systems and scripts."* And within the last two years of my association with the rich people, I discovered that many of them did not get rich by luck as is commonly perceived, but because they chose to be rich, and worked towards it. So anyone can be rich and happy – if they want to be.

I go back again to my past…

I was born from humble beginnings when parents had not much education and my father did not have a regular job, and when traditional mothers, did not work, but stayed home to take care of the family, and do all household chores. On top of that, there were eight brothers and sisters in the family, of which I was the sixth . At age nine, I was helping my eldest sister sell fish at the market. I was asthmatic, always sick and very thin, but despite that illness, I learned to work very hard from a very young age. When I was in high school, my next eldest sister, started a garments manufacturing business right next to the kitchen and living room of our house. After her elementary education, she worked as a dressmaker in my uncle's garments factory and soon enough, she started on her own business. I was about 13 years old then, just starting high school, yet had so much work experience already.

I helped my sister in all areas of her business – dressmaking, sorting, buying fabrics and other materials, selling at her stores, delivering finished products – and just anything and everything. I grew up with the harsh realities of life, struggling and working hard to make a living and survived the hard way.

My elder three brothers also started working at an early age, and also, did not either start or finish high school. So, at a young age, I was wondering if this trend would continue and if I would be the next in line, as I was about to finish high school. Then, I would have the same fate, and life, as my parents and brothers and sisters. In that small town, where girls, at a young age married fishermen, there were many children living in poverty and deprivation. I was not going to let this happen to me - I started to dream and imposed something to the universe…

I graduated from both elementary and high school, with honors despite my asthma from birth. My young mind had already decided that I would be different. I decided then that I would go to university, get a degree and a good job, and not marry early, or stay in this place where I grew up. I told myself, I will leave this place, go to the big city and other big places with greener pastures, explore the world and have a better life. Be happy. Be successful. Be rich. What else is there to achieve?

All of these happened, and at that time, who would tell me there was already a book, *Think and Grow Rich* by Napoleon Hill, that says "to grow rich, one must start with 'Burning Desire'"? - or that the power of my subconscious mind had been picked by the divine providence and the universe before I had even read Dr. Joseph Murphy's book on *The Power of the Subconscious Mind*?

And what happened to my two elder sisters – never studied after elementary, but conscientiously, patiently, industriously, and painstakingly had worked so very hard in the last 50 years, that they became very successful and happy, too.

During those formative years of helping my two elder sisters in their businesses, I was regularly going to Manila. It gave me opportunities to meet well-dressed, rich people who own their own businesses, and professionals and executives, working in big companies in tall buildings. I saw their big houses with swimming pools, nice cars and fancy lifestyles. But, they looked very simple and did not act like rich people. I admired and idolized them and thought, I would like to be like them – simple, rich, successful and happy.

I also could not forget how being poor and having no money could give me so much motivation to work so hard to get out of that poverty. There was a time when I had to pay my university tuition and my parents did not know where to get the money. My father went to my aunt, who was my mother's younger sister, and for whom, my father was working for as a fishpond caretaker to borrow as an advance from his salary. To my father's surprise, this aunt of mine would not lend him the money. He was so mad, he got a big bolo (a big knife) and attempted to kill my aunt. This caused a rift between our families and that has stuck in my mind. My father did this out of his love for me, and because I had the strong desire to study. I am not letting this get in the way. I worked at my sister's garments factory after school, and during school breaks. This taught me how to work long hours, work very hard and save money - so that we do not have to beg for money, like my father did. I did not want to be embarrassed again, or have a member of the family try to kill someone, or cause a rift among family members. Because of this, my desire to succeed just got stronger.

My parents never imposed their children to study. Maybe they thought, they could not afford it, so why impose? Or maybe, because they themselves never pursued higher education and it was okay to live that kind of life. Remember what I said - I have decided that I will change my life no matter what and whatever it takes – at all costs! I am responsible for my own future, happiness and success!

As I started to work and made money early in life, I recognized the value of labor and money. And because of my burning desire to make something out of myself, I have developed these habits that unconsciously and unknowingly became a part of me. These are the habits I had learned and developed, from when I was young, to my adult years, and found very helpful to my life and success. These are my most important, good habits that worked very well for me, and, I would like to pass them on to my children, grandchildren and great grandchildren and maybe, you as well, can pick up something good from them.

"Early to Bed and Early To Rise Makes a Man Healthy, Wealthy and Wise"

- from the famous Chinese philosopher Confucius, that is what I did. They say, you are either a morning person, or you are not. In my family, we were all morning, afternoon and evening persons; it does not matter the time of day, for we all work from dawn, and stopped working only when we had to. Working at the market in Manila, helping my eldest sister, we woke up at two to three in the morning, to get the fish in the fish port and bring them to the market. And because, we had to wake up that early, my mother and sister would prod me to also go to sleep early. This experience trained me to be punctual and prompt. As I went to the university in Manila, and commuted by public transport, I had to wake up at 4:30 in the morning and leave the house at 5:30 am to be at my 7:00 am class: there was less traffic and hassles, as everyone else was rushing. And Manila, if you still do not know, is one of the worst places for traffic in the world. Habits, as they say, once formed are hard to break; so that is the reason why I am almost always early, and would hardly ever be late for any class, work, meeting, appointment or deadline. As I was hired later by an American multinational company, whose character for being on time is known for, my being prompt and punctual was more ascertained, and gave me so much comfort and benefits.

And why does going early work for me? Because, firstly, I avoided the traffic. Secondly, I have the freshest mind in the morning when I first wake up, so I am productive at work or study. Thirdly, I avoided the stress of rushing; when I am late for work or school, I am so embarrassed, and do not feel good about myself when I go in late. And fourth, I have some time to organize my day, and to plan and think about what I will do for that day. Lastly, if I have gone in early, then I can finish my work early, and can go home early. Then, I can do whatever I want with my life, like go to the gym, go to the mall or just relax at home, or be with friends outside, or simply read a book.

I know, nowadays, people have afternoon shifts or evening shifts, and are used to going to sleep late, and waking up late, too. Some of my kids are just used to sleeping so late, if they do not have to wake early for work. I would think that it is best to go to sleep at the right time, even if not early and wake up earlier, so you have time to pray, plan your day, or even to go for a walk or go to the gym. Regular sleep patterns are part of the health habits that I will talk about in other parts of this book.

"Save Your Pennies for the Rainy Days"

During those days, money was hard to make for my parents, who were not rich and had no regular source of income. I had an ambition to study, and finish my education. The only way I could do that was to save money for my tuition and school expenses. Every summer break from school, I would work at the university as a teller during enrollment periods as well as working in my sister's garment factory. I was also writing for the College of Commerce, at the university where I studied, which gave me a stipend for every article I wrote. At 17 years old, I opened a bank account in which to put my savings. Before that at about 13-16 years of age, I was making money, and kept it in the closet, only to find out one day, that someone has stolen it. I learned my lesson, so when I was already in Manila for my university degree, I opened a bank account without even my parents knowing about it.

Why do we have to save money? First, we need money for our emergencies and necessities. We would not have to borrow and beg, just like the experience that I told you about earlier. Second, we need money for our education and improvements. I finished my university partly due to my working part-time, and saving my earnings. Third, we would have money to travel and go to places where we can enjoy some luxuries.   When I was small, going to the city to watch a movie, or eat in restaurant, was a big deal. Back then, I could have new clothes for Christmas and during Easter Sunday. Fourth, having savings gives us security. We saved money before we could build our own house, or buy a car, jewelries or new clothes. We did not have credit cards. We did not apply for a mortgage. We were afraid to borrow for fear of interest, being rejected, or simply scared of debt itself.

"Spend Less Than What You Make"

The corollary is to save, save, save. I also developed the habit of spending less than what I make, or earn.   If I have to have a certain amount of money for my studies, I have to save. I also did not want to ask money from my parents, whom I saw were already struggling to provide food, shelter and clothing.   I thought, I should always have money in the bank for whatever I really need, without asking or begging. With this belief and habit, I have never run out of money, from age 17 until now.

Nowadays, with the advent and prevalence of credit cards, and all forms of debts that are available, people are indebted, and continue to drown and have no idea when they can ever get out of debt. Currently, the Canadians are indebted 1.65 times of their income on the average.

"Study, Get Good Grades, Get A Good Job and You Will Have Security in Life"

This was the old belief that my parents and family have impressed upon me. So when I graduated from the university, passed my CPA (Certified Public Accountant) exams, and got an accounting job in an American multinational company in the Philippines' financial district, I thought all my dreams had come true, and I should be okay for the rest of my life. And when I was working as an accountant, I continued to study and advance in my career. I even started to pursue an MBA (Masters of Business Administration).

At the present time, this may no longer hold true, as being happy and successful no longer hinges on getting a degree from a university. That job, that we used to love, may not guarantee that much success and security. As I have experienced myself, my first big earnings in real estate were a product of a few days' work; I would have had to struggle for two years as an Accounting Manager, in a multinational company, to earn the same amount. But, it doesn't mean any Tom, Dick or Harry can do it, because not every Tom, Dick or Harry had my childhood experience of hard work, industry and resilience, and the mental aptitude to quickly make decisions at the right time, or focus on a solution rather than the problem. Every powerful, good habit and trait, ingrained in one's persona comes in handy when the opportunity appears in front of you.

"Set Your Goals"

Dreams and ambitions to reach have to be anchored on goals and specific tasks. Or they will remain as dreams and wishes and we blame why luck has not come into our life. In my career, I learned budgeting, forecasting and how to analyze variances against actual results. I have learned and applied planning, organizing, coordinating, delegating and controlling. I have learned to set goals and measure my performance against these goals. These work experiences and disciplines inherently integrate in my character and personality, and therefore, also, in my personal life.

I had then started and learned setting goals for :

1. **Career** – continuing education, getting promotions every year or two,
2. **Travelling** – go to places I want to go to, locally and internationally
3. **Investing in myself** – through seminars, education, proper grooming
4. **Keeping healthy and slim** – through proper diet, exercise
5. **Organizing the home** – housekeeping and managing the home
6. **Family life** – getting married, having children, divorce and separation

I am happy to share, in the following chapters, what I believe are the most helpful 12 habits to a happy and successful life…

CHAPTER 1
HEALTH IS WEALTH

*"A healthy body and mind and soul rests a chance
for more happiness and success."*

Unless you are healthy, it may be a struggle to be happy and successful. Health and happiness and success are intertwined and have a direct link. And I mean health not only physical, but also mental, emotional and psychological. We have seen very rich people who have terminal illnesses and their money can not help them, despite all the medicines and latest medical technology they can afford. Money does not matter anymore when emotions are involved - like dealing with deaths, separation and grief. And, if you are suffering from a debilitating illness such as cancer, arthritis, schizophrenia, Parkinson's disease, or Alzheimers's, then it becomes very challenging to achieve success and happiness.

Health is the number one ingredient required in order to have success and happiness. After all, one needs a healthy body, mind and soul to achieve success and happiness.

How do we try to achieve health? Here are my best bets, which may be the same as most other people's:

1

Eat Healthy

Healthy eating can affect mental and emotional health. Eating right can help maintain a healthy weight and avoid health problems. It can also affect mood and sense of well- being. Eating an unhealthy diet has been linked to obesity, disease, stress, depression, anxiety and mental disorders.

There are so many tips and advice on what to eat, and there can be conflicting and opposing views. I am not a dietitian or a doctor; these are my personal opinions. If you have a medical problem, you need to consult a doctor for your proper diet. Here are some of my personal healthy eating habits:

1. **Eat more fresh fruits and vegetables**
   Fruits and vegetables are low in calories and they are packed with vitamins, minerals, antioxidants and fiber. Eat fruits for dessert, and vegetables as snack.

2. **Reduce your intake of sugar, bad fats and salt**
   Sugar creates weight problems and causes diseases like diabetes.
   Bad fats can increase the cause of certain diseases.

3. **Prepare more of your own meals**
   You know exactly what is in the food and can control what goes in your food.

4. **Read the labels**
   We should be aware of what's in the food so that we are warned how many nutrients, calories, sugar or fats are there, and we can decide whether we should eat that food.

5. **Drink plenty of water**
   Water helps flush our systems of waste products and toxins and decrease the chance of acquiring illnesses because of dehydration.

6. **Eat in smaller portions**
   This will allow you to digest the food faster and help control weight.

7. **Eat a healthy breakfast**
   It will jumpstart your day right, especially since the body does not take food the whole night while sleeping.

8. **Avoid eating at night**
   We are no longer active at night, and giving the digestive system a break can help regulate weight.

9. **Avoid junk food and processed foods**
   This includes chips, sugary food, and sugary drinks; they have so much harmful preservatives, and so much fatty sugar that can cause obesity, and illnesses.

I have learned to eat healthy foods. When I was young, I was asthmatic and thin, and I was not eating fruits and vegetables. When I trained myself to like, and learn to eat fruits and vegetables, the asthma just went away, after 23 years. Just incredible! And from then on, I enjoyed life more and spent less on medications. I had more energy to go to the gym, I engaged in sports activities and I improved my posture.

Another experience I want to share is when I was in Los Angeles, California I got hooked and addicted to eating Doritos chips. I ate them everyday from morning to evening. My weight soared and I looked like a pig. The sodium and preservatives were so high, it could have ruined my kidneys. When I stopped, I went back to my regular weight; I was slim again and I felt a lot better about myself.

Exercise

We are referring here to physical exercise. Why is this important to happiness and success? We need to exercise to be physically fit and healthy, and it gives the following benefits:

1. Strengthens our muscles and cardiovascular systems
2. Boosts the immune systems
3. Helps prevent stress and depression
4. Helps promote self-esteem and physiological well-being
5. Helps maintain healthy weight
6. Helps avoid diseases like heart disease, cardiovascular diseases, diabetes and obesity
7. Helps improve mental health

Again, I am not a doctor, or a physical fitness trainer. If you have medical conditions, you should consult the medical practitioners.

I have been exercising for the last 37 years and I must say, this has helped me immensely in maintaining a very good weight, avoiding sicknesses, managing stress and keeping my sanity. Whenever I stop exercising, I will experience all kinds of pain, such as neck pain and back pain and I can easily become irritable. With regular walking, zumba classes, body toning exercises and yoga, I am almost always positive in my world and successes just come naturally. Back home in the Philippines, I was a lifetime member of Slimmers. Here in Canada, I am a member of a community gym center and go regularly four to five times a week, for aerobics classes. I also joined a meet-up walking group at Riverwood Park, where I enjoy nature walking, and meet new people and making new friends. Doesn't that make you want to be healthy and happy, too?

Sleep and Rest

We need the correct amount of sleep and rest, depending on age and medical conditions.

We are also all different and the amount of sleep needed may vary by individual. We need sleep so that the brain will be able to reorganize data for our thinking and learning. During sleep, the body has a chance to replace chemicals and repair muscles, other tissues and aging or dead cells. I am not a doctor and these are based on reports I have read. Insufficient sleep, according to what these reports also say, may cause serious health problems, such as heart disease, diabetes and obesity. We also tend to be in a better mood and have better weight control and clearer thinking, if we have enough sleep.

I personally can not think and function properly if I sleep less than 6 hours. I also tend to be moody and can not make a good decision if I am lacking sleep. So, these definitely are not making me happy, neither can they be helpful to making me successful.

See Your Doctor and Dentist Regularly

Many sicknesses could have been diagnosed, detected and treated in time if the person had gone to his doctor or dentist in time. A regular check-up and visits to the doctors should be a part of your annual or semi-annual routine. The reality is that people tend to be lazy about going to their doctor, or just take their health for granted. If they do not feel wrong about their body, they will not make a schedule to go to their doctor. They wait until something is wrong. The problem, for some, is that it may be too late to cure an illness that has been there for some time, or it may take longer to cure, because it has gotten worse from never being attended to. I regret how I was so scared and lazy to go to the dentist, that I went only when it was already so painful, that the dentist had to pull it out. Now I have lost so many teeth, and have had to have expensive options, and they are not as good as the original teeth.

"Don't Live in the Past, The Present is Here and the Future is Yet to Come"

This is more for our mental and emotional health. All of us have regrets or mistakes, committed in the past. Do not fret over it. Do not consume yourself about it. Just let it go. Look at what it has done for us. We surely learned good lessons from it and become a better, stronger person. Without the past, we do not know as much how to deal with the present, and hope for tomorrow. Here's why we should live in the present, more than in the past:

1. It broadens our mind because we are willing to accept new experiences, thoughts and ideas. If we are trapped in the past, we run from everything out of fear, anxiety, anger and other negative outlooks.

2. Awareness of the present stops us from putting conditions on achieving success. If we say, "If I go to Europe, I will be happy". This implies that if it does not happen, we are vulnerable to feel failure and unhappiness.

3. By being present now, we have more time for our social network and growth.

4. We are not distracted, so we can be more persuasive and we sound confident and in charge. This leads to more

successful business endeavors and fruitful relationships –
both personal and business.

5.   Living in the now has a proven positive effect on mental and
     physical health. This eliminates the negative feelings about
     the past mistakes and fears of the future. Then we do not
     worry anymore, and stress is avoided. The absence of stress
     avoids anxiety and depression that can cause chronic
     diseases.

As we say, 'Forgive and forget'.

If we can not deal with forgetting the past, such as trauma and
a difficult past, we can seek professional help and we can be
happy again.

Living in the present allows us to live longer, happier and fuller
lives.

Have Fun, Will Travel

Travelling to my favorite dream destinations, before I die, are
on my bucket list. This is a sure secret to happiness and success.
Generally, this is my way of rewarding myself and recharging.
From my personal experiences, these are the benefits of
travelling:

1.   **It broadens our perspective.** Seeing other people's lives in
     other places, we become more appreciative, and thankful for
     the life we have. We come to evaluate our own values.

2.   **We learn to live in the moment.** Being at the Eiffel Tower
     overlooking the River Seine in Paris or having a night cruise
     on the Danube River just makes us stop and live in that
     moment. Nothing feels better and more rewarding.

3. **We value experience, over things.** When I got hooked on travelling, I started saving for the next trip and gave less to other material things, so that I can travel again. Travel becomes a way of life.

4. **Learn to go with the flow.** I used to get easily upset when things did not go my way. When I started travelling more, I learned quickly that I can handle most situations that are not worth getting upset about.

5. **We become more open to different ways of life.** We learn to value and appreciate different cultures, people and their differences, and that everyone and every place, has their own beauty and goodness.

6. **I became closer with my Creator,** knowing how lucky I am for having been given the opportunity to travel, and knowing that God is so good, He created such beautiful places.

7. **Anyone has the opportunity to see and enjoy the world.** This world is such a beautiful world and there is so much to be thankful for.

8. **We become renewed,** and whatever problem or issue that is bothering us, we seem to have a more positive outlook, and a solution, when coming back after travel.

Heal From Emotional Pains

As human beings, we all experience emotional pains in our lives. This is inevitable.

Here are some of what I have personally experienced, and how we should deal with it:

1. **Rejection** – can come from people, prospective clients, employers or anyone. We can not please everybody. We can not expect everybody to like us. When I was new to Canada 13 years ago, I was almost giving up when after hundreds of job application letters, I was getting few interviews, and nobody was hiring me. I learned to improve my resume and to find other sources for work. I never gave up. Then one day, I got a job. "A winner never quits and a quitter never wins".   So just keep going tenaciously, and one day, somebody will love, and say yes to you. Then you will become happy and feel so successful.

2. **Loneliness** – This happens when we are alone, rejected, or when we have separations or strained relationships. The key is to have acceptance and a positive attitude, and move on. For some, they may need professional help. For some, all they need is time, and they can move on again. What I do is exercise, read inspirational books or talk to someone - and pray and talk to God.

3. **Guilt** – This happens when you can not let go of thinking that you committed wrong, or wronged a person.   To overcome, you can apologize to that person, and forgive yourself completely.

4. **Disappointments** – Over people, loved ones or events, in expectations not happening, can all take a toll in one's life. You can focus on other things or look at the lesson, to see what's positive from this event not happening.

5. **Failure** – Yes, it can hit your self-esteem. You may get support from people you love and trust. You can also look at the good things that come out of this failure, like learning a lesson, or what can be done instead, next time.

6. **Loss of a loved one** – Mostly when a loved one has died. I have experienced the loss of both parents, and my three brothers. It is painful, no matter how prepared we are for their death, even if we have been expecting it. For when you lose a loved one, it is always painful. Time and acceptance will help us until we ourselves accept our own mortality, and that our own time will come.

Let us take care of ourselves, maintain healthy habits.
We deserve to live to the fullest and be happy.
And when we are happy, it is easier to be successful.

CHAPTER 2
NEVER STOP LEARNING

"Knowledge is power"

I used to hear from my parents when I was young, "If you study, no one can take away that knowledge that you acquire. It can not be stolen, can not be swept away by fire, flood, or earthquake. It's all yours and your only capital in life."

So, despite all adversities in life – lack of money, asthma, distance of university from home to Manila, I strived to study and finished my university degree. "If there's a will, there's a way." "Nothing is impossible under the sun."

Because of my strong ambition to finish a university degree and use this as a capital to a bright future as my mother said, I made it happen. I started my schooling at seven and a half years old. No prep, no kinder. We had no money and I had to study elementary in public school. I was a very diligent student and so, I graduated with first honorable mention. My adviser told me I should have been salutatorian, but I had more absences than present days, and skipped a lot of exams. Everyone has our own motivation; that is why we do things. And from that goal or ambition, habits are acquired without our conscious effort, because we are only driven by our desire.

I would like to share the various ways and sources of learning and education.

University Education

This is the traditional way of getting formal education and is perceived to be the best way to succeed in life. It is also believed that university graduates get better jobs and earn considerably higher income than non-graduates. They are also most likely to stay in employment. People with university education have mental disciplines that can help them achieve success, because they have developed persistence, good study habits, patience and resilience.

Going through university was a lot of hard work, as you have to study, and study for many subjects, for many semesters, for at least four years. You have to prepare for regular tests, preliminary exams, final exams and a thesis as a requirement to graduate. There are homework and projects. You need a lot of money. In my case, because money was scarce, I had to work part-time and deprived myself of many things in life that I shelved aside, like not buying clothes, and being content with hand me downs, buying used books instead of brand new, sacrificing the hardships of public commuting instead of staying in dormitories, and many more.

My own university education at the University of Santo Tomas in Manila, Philippines has taught me many things. Completing two majors in Business Administration – Entrepreneurship, and Accounting - has allowed me to learn formal subjects in business and, that became useful when I started my real estate business later in life. Also, it was easy for me to get a good job, in an American multinational manufacturing company. Landing a good job in a very good company, afforded me to build my career, and develop myself to become a professional, and enjoy the good times of friendships, travel and camaraderie. Being a professional, you also meet other professionals, and same-minded people in your career. My university education forced me to have the habit of always studying and analyzing things, to be alert and effective, and continue to hunger for knowledge and discoveries. My personality blossomed to a better and more learned person. I was travelling life openly, and welcoming new opportunities. Life started to become good, and the journey of life became more exciting.

Getting a Professional License and Passing Board Exams

Having a professional license and passing board or national exams, gives you an edge or advantage, over a university graduate, who does not have it. Serious studies, dedication and hard work, are mandatory so that you are assured to pass the exams. Plus, you have to spend time and money to study and review. And again, you somehow have no life, especially if you are working at the same time. Because of the competition, and the requirements now of many companies to hire a professional licensee, as opposed to a regular graduate without license, it becomes much easier to get a good job and higher salaries. A license or certificate becomes your passport to getting a good job, higher position and more decent pay.

Soon after my college graduation, I reviewed for the Certified Public Accountants (CPA) Exams, as well as Career Eligibility to work in the Philippine government. I passed both. I did not work in the government, as I decided to work in a private company. When I retired from that company, to focus on family life, I took the Real Estate Licensure exams and became a Licensed Real Estate Broker in the Philippines. In Canada, I studied CGA (Certified General Accountant) up to the advanced level. Then, I studied real estate for six months after my work hours and took the exams and became a licensed real estate agent. My being a CPA has earned me a lot of money, and the real estate licenses, in both the Philippines and Canada, has earned me, even more money.

At the present time, there are many areas of specialization where one can study, and get a license for shorter periods of time, and not cost a lot of money. Choose one that you are interested in. Make sure that you also study about the field that you are considering, to see if there is a bright prospect for you to stand out and excel in this field, and really like to do it. As they say, a job is not a drudgery, and you are happy, if you love what you do.

In my accounting career, I was truly enjoying it, as it was very fulfilling when I was advancing in my career, and seeing the fruits of my hard work. I developed the habits of focus, perseverance, tenacity, punctuality, professionalism, speed and problem solving ability. The spartan training that I acquired from my first employer, Union Carbide Philippines, Inc. (now Energizer), taught me many positive habits and attributes that brought me to many other companies who have always liked the way I worked. Honesty and integrity were also tested in time, and became embedded in the person that I have become.

Professional Memberships and Associations

Professional associations are usually nonprofit organizations for the purpose of furthering a particular profession and the interests of the individuals engaged in that profession and the public interest.

Being a CPA in the Philippines, I became a member of the Philippine Institute of CPA's (PICPA). As a member, you pay membership dues for getting membership benefits such as receiving member journals, updates in the profession, educational materials and fellowships with other members, and special deals on conferences and seminars.

As a real estate broker, also in the Philippines, I was a member of the local board , the Cebu Real Estate Board, which administered the Licensure Exams to get my license as a Real Estate Broker. We met once a month and this gave us the opportunity to network with other real estate brokers. We also exchanged our listings, since the MLS (Multiple Listing Service) was not yet introduced.

Professional association memberships are beneficial for your own professional development, and for the future of your career or business. Connections and relationships are built, and can be very valuable for success.

Short Term Courses or Certificates

If you are not interested in going through the long years of the expensive and laborious university education, you can choose to take short courses, that are as short as one month, three months or six months. If you select the right one for yourself, and work through it with all your heart and mind, you can be as successful, or even more successful than a university graduate. I have seen it happen many times to so many people. Examples are my own two sisters, and my second degree cousin, who are in the garments business. They only finished elementary education, but they are richer than many university graduates. They have worked their way up through hard work, dedication, sacrifices, working very long hours, paying their debtors on time, excellent customer service, fairly priced products and delivering what they promise. These people have become my inspiration and have also become my idols; I strive to have the same traits as they have, only in different fields, and, definitely, in my personal life, too.

Nowadays, there are many short term courses where you can get a certificate that can land you in good jobs, and high pay. Or they can lead you to have your own business, and be a millionaire.

Be the Best in Anything That You Do

May I share with you one of the secrets in succeeding, in either employment or business?

Be different. Be the best. Give more than 100%.

"Get out of the sea of sameness and be in the island of individuality."

It doesn't matter what you do. Just be the best in that field.

How do we know if you are? When people look for somebody who can help with their problem, or need some product or service, you are the first person they think about.

When I was an area sales director in Fil Estate Realty Corp. in the 1990's, I became the number one sales director in Fil Estate Realty Corp., as well as in the whole five marketing companies. I sold 52 shares of Fairways and Bluewater proprietary shares in just one month. Fairways and Bluewater is a multi-billion peso real estate project in Boracay, Philippines with five star villas, golf courses, hotels and other first class amenities. When this project was introduced, I got so excited, it sunk into my head and heart, and I fell in love with the project. I went to every presentation and launching. I studied the project with my husband, ordered sales materials and planned our strategy. I contacted the top five real estate brokers in Cebu, Philippines, organized a meeting and presented the project in a nice hotel.

These brokers themselves bought the shares and recruited more
and more and sold more and more. It created a ripple effect. I
made so much money, got so many awards, and became very
popular; I was called the "Queen of Fairways and Bluewater".
I became known in the industry, and other real estate marketing
companies would come to me to offer me positions in their
company.

Be different and your success and happiness will also be
different!

Surround Yourself With Like-Minded People

There is a saying " Tell me who your friends are and I will tell
you who you are."

This is one of the secrets of success and happiness.

Whoever you spend most of your time with, you will adopt their
attitudes and their self -esteem. You will even start earning the
same income, or close to their income. Your environment shapes
and influences your life. If you want to be happy, be with happy
people. If you want to be rich, be with rich people. They do
not have to be popular. It could be a friend, or someone you
know, who can help you to be the person you want to become,
and who can guide you on your journey. If you want to be
successful in a particular area, be with people who have been
successful in that area. Start networking with established people
who share your dreams.

And on the other hand, don't surround yourself with toxic and
negative people who don't add value in your life. They are
contagious, and badly influence you towards failure and misery.

Get a Mentor

All my life, I have never seriously thought of having a mentor. Why would it occur to me? Are not my parents, sisters, brothers, teachers, professors, seminar leaders, priests, guidance counsellor – not enough to be my mentor? Is mentorship just an extra cost that will just repeat what I can read in books, or watch on webinars?

By a stroke of fate, I got a mentor in 2015. I have been wanting to invest in US properties since the US recession in 2008. I bought an expensive mentorship in the US and spent a lot of money attending their seminars in Las Vegas and Florida, I looked at so many properties, not buying a single one. Then in 2011, I formed my corporation, and also family corporations to jointly purchase US properties. I got a realtor in the Florida area, who also showed us properties and whenever we would make an offer, it was no longer available. I just got frustrated and so we decided to stop thinking about this idea.

Four months after having a mentor, I bought four single family homes – two in Florida and two in Ohio, all join ventures with my mentor. They are giving me positive cash flows. I also bought a piece of land in Florida. I could not believe how easy it was to buy real estate in the US. How I got funds, and how I did it, is a subject that needs a separate discussion.

I meet with my mentor about two times a month. Having a one on one meeting with my mentor is giving me more and more personalized education, helping me to overcome fears and giving me more confidence. He has actually done real estate investing in Canada and the USA. He shared with me his failures and successes, and patiently taught me to avoid pitfalls, what to do and what not to do, like a hand in my hand. His inspiration and motivation are enough for me to be more courageous, and to move forward without fears. I was reading books I was not reading before. Like *Think and Grow Rich*, I have read three times, *The Power of the Subconscious Mind, The Secret, The Monk Who Sold His Ferrari,* and so many more. He taught me about listening to audios - morning and evening - affirmations, writing my goals, doing my success board, improving my linked in profile, and many more things. With my mentor, I learned not only to be with same minded people who I wanted to become, but how to be rich and happy. He became my accountability partner, advisor, confidante and friend. Most of all, I learned from him, that we can be rich, if we choose to be, and there is a way to do it. And, that is what I learned to teach other people, as well, who want to be rich, successful and happy.

CHAPTER 3
STAY POSITIVE

"Positive thoughts produce positive results"

Life is not a bed of roses. We all go through ups and downs, sorrows and joys, successes and failures. Not everything goes the way we want it and life can be challenging at times. For some, frustrations, disappointments and worse – can be a trauma.

How we react and handle ourselves in difficult situations spell the difference between rising triumphantly or drowning in misery. I choose to be triumphant. I must admit, as human beings, it is not easy and is easier said than done. Just like in anything, practice makes perfect. The more hard situations we experience and the better we deal with every situation, we get better and better.

With all of what I have personally gone through in life, I have learned that I must be bigger than the problem. If I let the problem be bigger than me, I lose, and become very unhappy. I now choose to be happy.

Becoming strong to life's harsh realities takes time and maturity. It comes with age, and depends on your attitude and strength. It is a journey to getting better at it. Let me share with you some ways to stay positive.

The Power of Gratitude

Being thankful and grateful and showing appreciation is very powerful. Regardless of one's religious belief, gratitude, when done in prayers, is a spiritual way, and one of the best ways, of finding the presence of God. If we cultivate the habit of gratitude, we become happier, less depressed, less stressed and more satisfied with our lives in general, and with our social relationships in particular. We have more positive ways of coping with difficulties that we experience in life. We do not resort to negative coping strategies like going on drugs, and alcohol, running amuck or become mentally deranged. Gratitude has been proven to be the parent of all other virtues and increases well-being.

How do we practice gratitude?

1. **Gratitude Journal** – I have learned to write five gratitude statements everyday. I do it every evening before I go to sleep, just after thinking what I did for the day, and what happened during the day. I write something like, "I thank you for my dog Calvin" or "I thank you for giving me my grandson Leon". You can write anything. Then you can sleep in peace.

2. **Thank God every morning when you wake up.** This is the best way to start your day right. You wake up in joy, as you are alive and full of hope. You are energized and every morning is a new day that is all yours to enjoy and do something about.

3. **Say thank you all the time.** When we appreciate when something is done for us, big or small, it makes us feel so good. And it makes the receiver of your thanks, so much better. What a 'thank you' does is a lot more than you can

imagine. It multiplies exponentially, as when you hear someone say 'thank you' to you, you feel you are appreciated and this boosts your morale and encourages you to help that person more as you are being appreciated. Also, be specific when you say 'thank you' like "Thank you for your taking the time to do this for me." You can say 'thank you', in person, by email or text. Nothing is worse than when you do something for somebody, and he does not acknowledge it, or say 'thank you' in return.

4. **Send a 'Thank You' note or card.** This is a formal way of showing appreciation. The recipient getting a 'thank you' card will see the big effort made by the sender in getting that card and mailing it. Written notes as opposed to a verbal 'thank you', could have a bigger impact, and they can forever keep that note, or card, which can have everlasting effects and benefits.

The Power of Affirmations

Beautiful and meaningful affirmations are self-empowering and foster positive mental attitude. They can be written, and you can read or say them aloud. Or, they can be in audio format, or in video format and you can listen to it and repeat after every statement. They should be in present tense, positive, personal and specific. If done regularly, like morning and evening or anytime during the day, they help the user to re-program their thought patterns, and will produce positive effects. Choose positive words that are nourishing and uplifting, such as "I believe", "I can do it", "I will be" or " I intend to", and avoid words like " I hope ", or "but" or "I can't do it".

What you say is what you are, and what you will become, so choose positive statements and the whole universe will bring you all those positive results from what you are affirming.

Think good, and good follows. Remember, the universe does not filter and will only listen to your voice! I personally listen to audio for positive affirmations every morning when I wake up, and every evening before going to sleep. Here are samples of positive affirmations:

1. I have a burning desire to be rich, healthy, happy and grateful
2. I help others
3. I forgive
4. I forget the past
5. I am strong-willed, determined and persistent
6. Money is continuously circulating in my life
7. I will lose ten lbs. in three 3 months
8. Whatever I do, I will prosper

**For more samples of affirmations,
go to www.journeytoanewyou.com.**

Find Good Lessons and Benefits in Every Bad Situation

There are times when bad things happen to good people, like getting into a car accident - not your fault - or getting lost looking for a place or address. Our natural tendency is to react negatively or bitter about it. Some years ago, I got into a car accident, and was so upset about it. I had whiplash, neck injury and back pains. I went to therapy for more than a year. Then, later, on I recognized that there were good lessons to be learned from this accident. I should not be driving when I am sleepy, or not feeling well, and appreciate the fact that I survived the accident, and am still alive; I can still do things I want to do. I also reaped some benefits like the soothing massages, personal trainings, physio chiropractic treatments and aqua therapies that brought me back to good shape. Have the habit of finding the lesson in even the worst situation, instead of focusing on the problem . You will benefit from turning the bad event into a good opportunity, and always get the benefit from it.

Stop Complaining, Stop Criticizing, Stop Blaming, Stop Gossiping

I have seen people do nothing but complain and make justifications for their actions, mistakes and inabilities. Or, do nothing but criticize, blame and find fault with anything and anyone. While this world is not a perfect world, focusing on these negative habits can be toxic. If we constantly do this, our brains tend to gravitate towards the negative. It is like being bothered by the thorns on the stem of the rose instead of being marveled by the sight of the beautiful rose. If we are actually going through a really tough time, we can share these feelings with a close friend, or family friend, or we can see a therapist to talk about our negative feelings. If something is not going right, we can focus on how we can help, or find a solution, rather than complain. Then, if we are able to help find a solution, we are happier, and feel good about ourselves, and others feel good about us. Everybody is happy.

Find What Makes You Happy

Find your passion and what makes you happy. Follow your dreams, and work on it to become a reality. If we pursue a career or develop a hobby, it makes our life worthwhile; use our time wisely and we become happy. It can be learning how to knit, or enrolling in a new course that you like, or even volunteering. Whatever it is, we can also find our purpose in life. If we pray for guidance, and meditate on what it is that we can do best, we will be shown the way. When I decided that I will get my real estate license in the Philippines, and in Canada, I had the opportunity to help so many people buy, sell or invest in real estate. It is giving me so much satisfaction to be able to help people with their problems in real estate.

Take Care of Your Relationships

People need people. We are social beings who need the support of people we love, and who loves us. Relationships are key to happiness and success. We all need the love and support of family members and friends. In business and work, we need meaningful and rewarding relationships, with clients, customers, suppliers, associates and other people helping our business. In my real estate investing, I need my mentor, realtor, lawyer, banker, mortgage agent, appraiser, home inspector, contractors and staff helping close the deals. As a real estate agent, I need my brokerage, fellow realtors, cooperating agents, and the power team members to close a sale or purchase. As an employee, I relate to my superior, subordinate, suppliers, customers and all the support teams in the company. We have to take care of all the people we have working relationships with, as they not only provide a happy life, but also an enriching and successful career.

How do we Take Care of Relationships?

Well, we have to spend some time with them. Especially during important events in their lives. We are there for them in good times and bad times. Some people are there for us, but only in our good times. Then we know, who are real to us. In the hypnosis audio that I listen to everyday called *Killing Your Fears* it says " We get back what we send out". If we are kind, people are also kind to us.

Smile

It is said that "It takes more muscles to frown than to smile". So, smile, and the whole world smiles with you; cry and you cry alone". "Laughter is the best medicine". Have you ever felt the difference between smiling and frowning, or the difference between laughing and crying? If we are down and troubled, call a friend, read a book, walk, exercise, do what makes you really happy. And in no time at all, you will get through it and move on to life at a new growth level. The more humor we can put in every adversity or challenge, the more we can embrace it and have an open mind. And the better we can handle any situation with vigor and strength. Nothing can beat somebody who faces every situation with calmness, confidence and a positive attitude. And, it makes us look beautiful, as peace and happiness radiates in our external looks.

Listen to Motivational Speakers

Listening to great motivational speakers on a subject that concerns you, is very educational, enlightening and uplifting. This is a very good substitute to reading, and feels more direct, as you can see the person in the video, as if he were talking to you. And these are free and available if you have a computer and internet access; they are on You Tube or downloadable CD's. The advantage of CD's is that your eyes are not tired from reading, and you can listen anytime while driving, eating, or doing anything. You can also watch them on TV, or even hear them speak in person. If you don't know of anyone regarding your subject of interest, just google them, and you will surely find several options. You may also get DVD's and watch them on TV, or on your computer. Examples of motivational speakers are Brian Tracy, Tony Robbins, Jack Canfield and T. Harv Eker.

Read Motivational Books

There are many motivational books that you can borrow from the library, or own if you like to keep reading it for your own benefit. They are also available online. The advantage of having a book is that you can take them everywhere, and read them when you do not have a computer or internet access. Reading a book is always educational, enriching, motivating and inspirational. This is also one of the best habits you can develop in your lifetime, and is a guaranteed source of happiness. The knowledge you will get from reading is power in itself. The lessons you will learn are valuable and you get it so easily and directly even if you do not have time to meet with an expert. My favorite motivational books of all time is *Think and Grow Rich, The Power of The Subconscious Mind, The Secret* and *The Monk Who Sold His Ferrari.*

CHAPTER 4
SET GOALS

*"Everybody has their own Mount Everest
they were put on this earth to climb"*

My own goals start with a dream. This is what I would like to achieve or become. This is what I would like to get done specifically, in a certain time frame.

I was asthmatic from birth, and I always felt weak; this illness has caused me so much suffering. I made a promise to myself to do everything to get over it, and be permanently healed. I made it a goal, and formed some action steps to make it happen. I studied about this illness and tried all medications, medically or otherwise. At age 23, after university, I started participating in sports, and regularly went to the gym. I went swimming. I also enrolled myself in an asthma course, at a hospital, to learn more about it. The course was delivered by famous pulmonologists and asthma experts. Then upon advice, I had an allergy test and avoided all that I am allergic to. In no time at all, my asthma went away. Then, life became easier, and what a big relief! I moved on with my life, with more enthusiasm and energy. I mastered asthma like a real doctor.

When I had my last baby, he was also born with asthma, and it was also severe. I could never forget when it was so severe at age two, I had to bring him to the emergency section of a hospital, and he had to be admitted, but with no available room,

I had to rush to another hospital. We were in the middle of traffic, and I could hear the breathing of my child, that I thought, was going to stop. At that moment, I thought, if anything happens to him, then I would blame myself, because I did not do enough. So, I drove like crazy down the road, moving so fast to the hospital to get my son admitted and ensure that he would be treated right away. So, again, I made it a goal that I would get his asthma to go away. I asked my sister, who is a doctor, who the best pulmonologists are. So, I went to a few specialists, and selected the one I liked best and stuck with her for my son's treatment. She recommended me to another specialist - in eye, ear and throat. This eye, ear and throat specialist suctioned my son's nose and from the lungs, took all the phlegm that was exacerbating his asthma. I religiously attended every visit and followed up with these two doctors. I invested in some medical tools so that he could get treated right at the onset of an incoming attack. At age five, my son's asthma was gone. My goal was accomplished.

Goals may be in small, medium or large. The large goals can be sliced into medium goals and the medium goals into small goals. The goals may originate from what you want to accomplish, because that is what you want for yourself. An example is what you want to become, like you want to buy your first house, or you want to own your first car. Or, it could come from a problem or a situation. Just like my asthma story, or my son's asthma story.

Goals we want to attain vary according to individual as we are all at different stages and our needs and wishes are different.

Goals may be in different categories:

1. **Personal**
   This is what you want to attain in your personal life, such as finding a life partner, getting married, having children or deciding where to settle. These personal goals are critical to one's happiness because if things happen with no plans, or happen out of force or coercion, then it is causing misery. A mistake in this area can be hard or emotionally challenging to correct.

2. **Career**
   This is what you want to be your occupation or work. This is what you do in your life as a source of income and enjoyment. The right career choice may spell the difference between success and failure. As it is said, as long you like and enjoy what you do, then work becomes, not work, but fun to enjoy. You can be a driver, a singer, a doctor, a writer, an accountant – anything. A successful career will definitely help in the attainment of other goals, and become a source of happiness and success.

3. **Financial**
   This is the amount of money you want to make, or the financial success you would like to attain. Your goal may be to make $200,000.00 this year or to be a millionaire in three years. Or to donate $10,000.00 to a charity of your choice. The realization of a financial goal allows you to pursue other goals in other categories, as discussed here. If you have the means, you have the power to do anything and be successful in it. While money can not buy happiness, it surely does help.

4. **Education**
    This is what you would like to accomplish in your education, or learning arena. You may want to finish a short course, a college degree or a university degree. You may want to get certified in accounting, or the field of your choice. It may be a simple hobby you want to learn, like cooking or knitting. Whatever it is, as long as you are educating yourself, improving yourself, and making something out of it, it is a big source of both success and happiness.

5. **Physical**
    This is your goal for your body that helps you to function well in life and be healthy. A healthy body leads to a healthy mind and a happier life. You can not overemphasize the importance of taking care of your body and yourself, as everything else in your life suffers if you are not healthy. Keep repeating that to be healthy, you have to eat healthy, have enough sleep and rest, do regular exercise and see your doctor and dentist regularly.

6. **Pleasure**
    "All work and no play makes a man dull" as the saying goes. As human beings, we get tired and exhausted if we keep on working with no stop and relaxation. We can enjoy life's little and big pleasures like walking, travelling, being with friends and enjoying their company, we recharge our mind and body, and we go back to our work more energized and more productive.

7. **Giving Back**
    This is one of the noblest goals one can do in life. In Maslow's Hierarchy of Needs Theory, this is the self-actualization stage. When one has satisfied his basic and self- realization needs, he moves up to the self-actualization

stage, which is the highest one. You may start with volunteering your time and talents to a charitable organization. Or you can start a mission or a project for the poor and destitute. Or you may donate cash or any valuable property. There are many people and entities looking for help, and if we are blessed, it is a duty to give back. And if you do, there will be more blessings.

Why Do We Set Goals?

Here are my main reasons for setting goals.

1. **Goals Keep You Forward**
    If you have a goal, you have a direction that will keep you going forward to attain that goal. You will set your mind to it, and that sets you to work towards it. I ask myself what I want to do this week-end. I say, I will go to the gym from 10-12 on Sunday, go to church on Saturday from 5-6, visit my grandson and daughter on Monday. If I do not put this in my head, then anything can just happen and I may not do any of these important things.

2. **Goals Help Big Goals to be Smaller and Attainable Goals**
    If you have big goals, and you write them down and plan them to be in certain time frames, they become more achievable. Say, you want to be a millionaire in 3 years. If you do not know how to become a millionaire in three years, this becomes only a dream. Then, you become discouraged, and lose your belief in yourself that you can become a millionaire. When you have a big goal and formulate a definite action plan and seriously work on it, then it becomes more attainable. Winning in a lottery, while you can become a millionaire, does not require so much goal setting and work, and, of course, it does not give you a big chance to accomplish that goal of becoming a millionaire. As it is said,

"When you have a goal, anything is possible. When you do not have a goal, nothing is possible."

3. **Goals Helps Us to Believe in Ourselves**
    When we have a goal, it builds an automatic belief and trust in ourselves, that we can do what we want to do and we can have what we want to have. When you write or say that goal, it is injected in the brain and it propels us to take action to make it happen. Once we start to doubt that it is possible, then it stays just a dream. As it is said "If you believe that it is so, then it is correct". So, we make sure that what we think, is always believing in ourselves. Say to yourself, everyday, many times a day "I believe in myself completely". "I believe that I can do this."

4. **Goals Hold Us Accountable for Failure**
    When we write our goals with timelines for achievement, it gives a powerful way to achieve it. When we see them at least when we wake up in the morning and before sleeping, then we are reminded. Then we get to evaluate or re-evaluate, if we are not on plan, or falling behind our goal. Then, we probably have to do something different and new, to be able to reach our goal.

5. **Goals Help Us to Know What We Want**
    When we reflect on our goals, it helps us to know what we truly want. Goals may come in different forms such as money, promotion, travel, or getting more titles in your name. This is critical because goal setting is like playing darts, in the way that if we do not hit the right spot, then we are aimlessly hitting it wrongly. Then, we become unhappy or unsuccessful, and have wasted our time and energy, then we have to re-set our goals. We also try not to be mistaken in thinking that happiness can only come from acquisition of material things.

Qualities of a Good Goal

1. **Attainable**
   A goal must be reasonably possible, or within reach. It is something within our means and capability. It is something that other people have done already. While you are aware that there are challenges and struggles, you believe you can do it. An example is when my goal was to pursue my education and have a university degree; I knew it was hard given our situation, but it was possible, and I did it. Despite adversities or challenges, we must believe that we can overcome these hurdles, rise up and fight over these and rise and be a victor.

2. **Specific**
   We should know what the goal will accomplish. It is certain, concrete, precise, definite, and clear. In my case, I knew what is the specific result, or accomplishment was necessary to finish my university degree.

3. **Measurable**
   The goal can be measured in definite terms. For example, like finishing an education is measurable. With a time frame and specific education criteria, it is measurable. In my own example, I completed my university degree, Bachelor of Science in Accountancy in the year 1990, for example.

4. **Time Frame**
   A good goal should have a definite time lines, or when it should be accomplished, such as becoming a millionaire by December 31, 2017. If we say my goal is to become a millionaire without a target time, then it is not clear. It may happen, or it may not happen. And if it happens, it may be years later.

5. **Realistic**

   Is your goal not out of this world? Does it make sense on it? Is it good for you, or to the intended party? Is it reasonable? Is it sensible? Is it within our talents, skills and capabilities? Is it relevant to you ?

How To Set Goals

1. **Think and Decide on your Goals**

   This is the first step in goal setting. We have to sit down and clearly, in our mind, ask ourselves, what we want in life. There are so many options and opportunities in life. They are up for grabs. The universe is waiting for us to ask and dictate what we want. What is our purpose and goal in life? Evaluate what we truly believe will make us happy, fulfilled and successful. Visualize it. On a higher level, what legacy do we want to leave behind to our children, family, and to the world?   You must have a burning desire to achieve that goal.

2. **Write Down Your Goals**

   Goals should be written down. You can make a vision statement and a mission statement. It is said that goals that are written down are more likely to be accomplished than if they aren't. When you write your goals down, the handwriting somehow travels into our brain and has an amazing effect of putting it consciously in our brain and working on that goal no matter what.

3. **Make a Vision Board**

   You may write your goals on a vision board along with pictures. You put the pictures of what you want to get in your life, or pictures of what you have just got and would like to get more of. When the US recession started in 2008, I knew I had always wanted to have the opportunity of buying at the lower prices, and I also knew that this opportunity may not happen again in my lifetime. I spent so much money, time and effort, but never bought a single property. In 2014, with the help of my mentor who taught me how to make a vision board, I was able to buy one property every month. In the first five months alone, since I made the vision board, I was able to buy 5 properties. For a sample of a Vision Board, go to my website, www.journeytoanewyou.com.

4. **Review Your Goals Frequently**
We must review our goals everyday to see if we are on track and if not, we can assess why we are falling behind, or not accomplishing our goals. Then we can do something more or be creative, or probably adjust our goals. If you consistently think about your goals, and conscientiously work on them, our conscious and subconscious mind, will work towards its accomplishment.

5. **Make an Action Plan For Your Goals**
Goals are just dreams and statements of what you want to do, unless you take action. Goals in order to be achieved, must be backed up with action plans and specific steps, with specific time frames. The action plans, and specific steps, should be thought out carefully and be moving towards the attainment of the goal. Just like when you are planning to start a new business, you have a business plan, budgets and feasibility studies. In your personal goals, you can do the same thing as it applies to your goal.

6. **What is the Reason for Your Goal?**
Know the reasons why you want to attain that specific goal. These reasons must be very good or noble. The reasons will fuel the achievement of the goal. The burning reasons for having the goal will drive us crazy, and we will do whatever

it takes to reach it. What drives your goal? Your children ? Your parents ? The poor kids in your country ? To give back to the community ?

CHAPTER 5
DISCIPLINE AND SELF-CONTROL

"Discipline is the bridge between goals and accomplishment"

The real world is full of temptations and any normal human being can succumb to it. We can also be impulsive to the 'spur of the moment' that can go against the realization of our goals. Discipline and self-control comes in either doing the best thing, or avoiding the wrong thing. Discipline is a learned behavior and it can be done at any point in your life. It is a behavior for life, that we should be conscientiously working at in order to continuously have success and happiness.

I have learned the power of imposed discipline, or self-discipline. I am accountable for my own life and success, nobody else is. If my parents did not impose upon me to pursue higher education, I can not blame them if I did not pursue it. I have learned to discipline myself until it becomes a habit, and a character is formed. If we find something is not working in our discipline, then we should change it as soon as we recognize it. We are responsible for our own fate.

So, if we are serious about achieving our goals, let us find out what are some of the areas where we can try to exercise discipline and self control.

Following Timelines and Schedules

Life is fast-paced for people with big dreams and goals. We deal with everyday life, with a 1,001 things to do. We focus on the urgent, most important ones for that moment in time, for that day, for that week, for that month, for that year, for that life. Many activities and tasks can be scheduled. We put time frames on these and adopt ways and means to ensure they are on schedule, so we can accomplish more and make sure important tasks are not missed. Then, they become a habit. We become efficient, save a lot of time, and as a result, become happier and successful. What can we do to make this happen?

1. **Daily To Do List**
    We make a daily list of things to do and with a specific time assigned to each task. We can do it in the morning or the night before, to plan our day for tomorrow. Then we check each of them off when done. If not done, we analyze why it was not done and work on it, either immediately or later when there is an issue with it.

2. **Block Time**
    We can block our time for a specific 'must do' activity or project. In real estate, we block our time for lead generation; that could be phone calling, door knocking or dropping off flyers. In my work now where I have so many emails and have no time to clean them up, I block one to two hours every Friday afternoon before leaving the office, so that it is clean before starting with the next week. If we do not block some time for important tasks, they can build up too fast. We must be strict in doing this, whether we want to do this or not.

3. **Use Calendar and Clock**
    This is an old way of putting our schedules on every day and
    date.   It can be in a physical calendar or by using our
    cellphone, iPad or computer. The present technology has
    allowed us to keep this in control including an alarm clock
    that will beep when it is time to do something.

Wise Use of Time

We used to call it time management. Some believe that, we do
not manage time - we manage only ourselves. However we look
at it, we must be aware that there are only 24 hours in a day,
seven days a week, 365 days a year and 12 months in a year. The
opportunities are vast, and many.   The resources are
tremendous and the technology is available to accomplish more.
All we need now is the wisest use of time. What can we do
about this?

1. **Avoid Time Wasters**
    When doing something, ask yourself if you have to do it.
    Does it help towards your goal? Does it make you happy?
    Is it necessary? When I was working in an American
    multinational company, we were asked to write all the tasks
    involved in doing our job. We had an industrial engineer
    that helped us with a time and motion study. I found out I
    was doing things I did not have to do. This helped me
    become more efficient, and faster in doing my job. This habit
    developed not only in my job, but in other areas of my life
    as well. As a result, I was able to do more and had more
    success; other people thought it was plain luck, or a miracle.
    They had no idea how much I worked in order to
    accomplish this.

2. **Learn to Say No**
   If somebody asks you to do something that you do not like
   to do, or it is against the realization of a goal, simply say no
   politely. In some instances, we are ashamed or do not want
   to hurt other peoples feelings, so we feel forced to say yes.
   Then, afterwards, it will cause us some problems or issues.
   We should mean what we say, and say what we mean. We
   become honest to ourselves, and to others. People will have
   more trust in us when we say no, and tell them the reason
   why, rather than say yes because we do not want to
   disappoint them or hurt their feelings. In the end, we end
   up not being able to do what we promised, and we knew it
   right from the start. We keep our integrity and honesty
   when we can say yes, and do it as promised, and say no
   simply because it is not possible.

3. **Multitask Smartly**
   Time is gold, and once lost, can not be recovered anymore.
   Some people say that multitasking is not effective because
   you can not do two things well at the same time. For me, it
   depends. When I am doing serious work, I can not be on the
   phone at the same time. But, if I am doing simple manual
   tasks such as filing or sorting documents, I can be on the
   phone at the same time. Common sense will tell us when
   we can multitask, since it depends on what we multitask,
   and on how well we can multitask.

4. **Allocate and Budget Time For Your Work**
   I always allocate and budget time for each task, or work. I
   do not have an eternity and there is such a thing as
   deadlines. In my work as an accountant, there are always
   deadlines such as when to file income tax returns, when to
   submit reports and when to close the month-end, or year-
   end. The world, and my world revolves around time. As a
   matter of fact, my life on this earth is time based – I get older

every minute and every hour of my time. In my work as a realtor, I have timelines to close the deal. In my work as a real estate investor, timing when to buy or sell is critical or I do not make money.

Spending

This is where many people fail as spending can be so enjoyable, that you are not thinking or not careful about it. In the present time, you can have as many credit cards as you want, and credit lines can be easily available. Merchandising and marketing campaigns are right in front of our face, tempting us to just buy whatever we want. It is said that spending has become a national pastime. We become more vulnerable to this temptation when we are under stress or are emotional. We are indebted more and more with bad debts for unnecessary and flimsy things. I have seen many people paying more interests on their credit cards when they pay only the minimum and taking longer time to fully pay them off, than they had imagined. Lack of control in this area can cause so much misery and failure. What can we do to improve spending habits ?

1. **Pay With Cash Instead of Credit Card**
    It is easier for us to spend when we are using the plastic card. Try leaving that plastic card at home and use cash instead when you are buying something. You will think twice, or thrice, before deciding to buy that item.

2. **Do Not Go to the Stores or Malls for Anything**
    If I do not want to spend or have no need for it, I do not go to the mall. When you are at the mall, you must be ready to spend. It is hard to resist the temptation when you are there. I say to myself, if I don't want to spend, I don't leave the house, or I do something more worthwhile.

3. **Make a Budget**

   One of the traits of successful people is that they make a budget. Just like when you are running a business, you should have a budget for expenses. I run my household like a business. I have a spreadsheet for the month with the daily accounting of what I spend. I also check my bank accounts daily to see what is going in and out of my account. Keep in control of your finances - this is one of the rules for success, not only in business, but also in one's personal life.

4. **Find Something Else To Do**

   When you have good hobbies or are wisely using your time, you do not have time to think of going to the mall or spending lavishly. Try reading books, or going to the library – there are tons of material you can read or listen to, or watch. Try going to the gym and exercise or going for a walk - these are healthy and therapeutic. Try forming a hobby – they are very fulfilling and can make you money.

Healthy Habits

This is a must for all. Healthy habits contribute greatly to a healthy body and mind. A healthy body and mind gives us peace. And peace brings happiness. And if we are healthy, we can do a lot of things for our success. A person with medical problems has limitations on what he can do, so success and happiness are also limited.

What are the ways we can develop good healthy habits?

1. **Eating healthy** – Eat more raw fruits and vegetables, and a balanced diet.
2. **Getting enough sleep and rest** – To recharge our bodies and

mind, we need enough rest and sleep. It is required to manage your energy effectively.

3. **Regular exercise** – Regular walking for at least 30 minutes a day or at least three to five days days in the gym doing aerobics, swimming, and machine exercises, will keep us fit.

4. Regular check up with the doctor and dentist – Just like preventive maintenance, our bodies need to be checked regularly to avoid illness, or prevent illness.

5. **Drink plenty of water** – This is required in order to flush out toxins and body waste.

Do Not Procrastinate

Do not delay what you can do today instead of tomorrow. Many people have the tendency to keep pushing things aside, because there is tomorrow and tomorrow after tomorrow. They do not like to be pressured, or they simply do not have a goal to finish a task, on a specific time and day. If this becomes a habit, there is no conscious effort to get things done on time. Then most likely, goals are never accomplished, if not delayed. Being punctual or prompt when getting to work or to appointments or when meeting deadlines is the same attitude you should have when you do not want to procrastinate, because you simply have that habit, and you will tend to do it in most areas of your life.

A person who is on time, and acts faster than ordinary, has more chances of succeeding and being happy. Developing the habit of speed, while not sacrificing quality of work and decision making, allows you to accomplish more which then, in time, that pays off in rewards and making more money.

Reward Yourself – Have a Break

It is not hard work all the time. You can have a balanced life, and enjoy what this life has to offer. Live life to the fullest. Life is short, and it passes by so quickly, we need to make sure we do not miss what we call "Life". We also have to celebrate life and our achievements in whatever ways we can afford or enjoy. These are the things I do to celebrate my hard work and successes, so I get more motivated to work harder for more successes:

1. Drink my favorite wine

2. Eat good food in nice restaurants

3. Wear nice, elegant clothes and jewelries

4. Go to the parlor for a massage, facial and make-over

5. Engage in new hobbies such as photography

6. Travel to new places

7. Make new friends, and new connections, that are positive and rewarding

8. Enjoy the company of my children and family members

9. Get in touch with old friends, and re-establish connections

10. Read and learn more

11. Go to the gym to enjoy zumba, body toning and yoga

12. Forget the bad past, enjoy the present and work for a better tomorrow

13. Listen to my morning and evening affirmations

14. Have a good, long sleep

15. Meditate

16. Commune with nature

17. Say thank you, and thank you and thank you for the blessings, successes and failures

CHAPTER 6
GO ABOVE AND BEYOND

*"If I do just what is expected of me, then I am just like
everybody else in the sea of sameness. I go above and
beyond to go to the island of differentiation."*

If we do exactly the same as the others where we do 100% of
what is expected of us, we are ordinary. In order to be
outstanding or distinguished in our field or in our goal
attainment, we have to do more than ordinary. Go the extra
mile. Be different way more than the rest.

You do more, no less. Do not cheat, lie or steal.

We go beyond the call of duty to ensure that every customer is
at least 100% satisfied. We truly need to stand out.

Andrew Carnegie said that the secret of his early success was
not asking what I must do for my employer, but "What can I
do?" He would never be contented to simply do what was
expected of him and leave it at that. He thrived on exceeding
both his own and others' expectations.

I believed in going above and beyond my own responsibilities
and finding ways to improve in business, work or anything that
I do, whether it is my duty or not. Do not think that a man has
done his full duty when he has performed the work assigned to

you. Promotion comes from exceptional work. Exceptional achievement comes from exceptional work.

I remember when I bought a house for my former boss. He got a loan from his company, and he had to submit the title of the property in his name so that he could get the loan (This was in the Philippines where I was a real estate broker). He was given two weeks or he would not get the loan. The titling of the property takes normally one month. I talked to all the people involved in the titling, from the one processing, typing the title, to the one checking, to the Register of Deeds who signed the title. I got the title all done in one week. I submitted the title to my former boss, who was very happy. He asked me how much the bill was and said he would issue me a cheque. When I told him my bill, he said he was expecting a higher fee because of the exceptional service that I had done for him. I was probably even happier than he was because I had done an exceptional job, and solved someone's problem. My superior, whenever possible, gave me good recommendations and referrals that brought me more business and money.

I learned early in my career as a real estate broker that when we serve our customers, we do not think about the money signs (PHP or $) first in our mind.

Many realtors back then would consider the money first, before serving their clients. From then on up to now, the customer is my priority and focus, to be served exceptionally, and have me go above and beyond their expectations, and because of this, all the money and goodwill just automatically follow.

We focus on our customer service and how well we can serve and protect the best interests of our client.

Always over-deliver in your product and service. If you do a little more, the future will take care of itself. The more we give, the more we get. Give first, and get after. That is the cycle that gives exceptional returns and benefits.

How do we go above and beyond? Here are some ways and examples among many.

As An Employee

1. You come early and leave late to learn more about and do more for your job. Regular employees arrive on the dot or late and leave on the dot, or earlier. When they are forced to extend work hours, it is a big deal and they complain about it. Extraordinary employees have the initiative and willingness without complaining, and take pride and are happy for doing it.

2. You have a concern for your employer and the company. You treat the company like it is yours. You find ways and means to save money and prevent losses for the company. Your actions and behavior supports this.

3. You deliver more than 100% customer service to internal and external customers. As a customer ourselves, we always remember the one who helped us with all their heart, who did the extra work and delighted us, and we will keep going back to that person as we enjoy his service.

4. You are honest and have integrity. You do not steal, lie or cheat. When you can be trusted, you get more opportunities, as people like you and want to work with you.

5. You have a team attitude; when somebody can not finish their work, or is sick or having problems, you step up and volunteer to help. It is "united we stand, divided we fall." We earn the respect of the team, it makes us a better person and it gives us a great experience.

To Your Clients

1. Highest standard of service or product
We give exceptional service, bonuses and more. We give complimentary, or trial services before we bill.

2. Fix problems
When there is a problem, we fix it promptly, and with a guaranty. If we can not fix it, we will replace or substitute, with an equivalent product or service, if not better.

3. Update the customer on the status of the service, project or order and on the expected completion or arrival time.

4. Give discounts whenever possible.

5. Send a note, or personally apologize for a delay, and tuck a gift, or something, as a token of this apology.

6. Find out what the customer wants and give it to him, whenever practicable.

What we focus on, expands. If we are customer service centered, we do extraordinary things, no matter how small, to delight the customers and make them extremely happy. A small gesture goes a long way. Be honest and be fair and we will win their loyalty and long-term business.

CHAPTER 7
LIVE WITHIN YOUR MEANS

*" There is no dignity quite so impressive and no independence quite
so important, as living within your means"*

This is an old adage that I still believe, up to the present time.
Many will probably disagree or have other ideas as nowadays,
credit is easy and one can be creative.

To "live within your means" means that you spend less than
what you earn. This is not easy to many. Nowadays, there are
so many credit cards, loans and emergency funds that allow you
to buy more things than your income would allow.
Unfortunately, that kind of lifestyle will catch up with you.

Spending less than your income is the foundation of personal
financial success. It seems like we can not get ahead in life if we
are spending more than what we make.

I grew up with a conservative view about money. I was brought
up with parents and family where if we do not have money, we
do not spend. Well, at that time, of course, credit was not
popular yet except borrowing from a relative or friend or buying
jewelry paid on installment.

With this principle of living within your means, is the principle
of delayed gratification. I developed the habit of not buying or
spending money on the "likes" and "wants"   until I had

acquired the "must haves" and "should haves". Like, if I am saving to buy my first house, I will cancel vacations and save the vacation money for the house. This is also following the priority principle in management. I would say, when I was struggling in life and money was scarce, I had to budget and prioritize. And until all the priorities where that scarce money is allotted for, I do not spend money for those things that are not necessary, but only "nice to have". When I graduated from university, I chose not to attend the graduation party, since my parents would have had to spend money to rent my graduation dress and toga and also pay for a picture. I also passed on the graduation ring, because it wasn't something I had to have in order to graduate.

Financial management is a must for a successful and happy life.

How Do We Live Within Our Means ?

Here are some ways that we can live within our means

1. **Make a budget**
    You do not need a sophisticated system to make one. I have been using a basic excel spreadsheet that lists my income and expenses on a daily basis. (For an example, go to www.journeytoanewyou.com). I track my income and expenses hand in hand with my online banking.

2. **Check and reconcile your bank accounts daily**
    You do this everyday to check against your budget on item 1, and see if the income and preauthorized payments are going in and out as per your budget. It will also remind you that you have to make a payment, either through online banking, or other ways of paying bills.

3. **Spend less money than income**

    Through budgeting, or even simply listing your income and expenses, you can analyze which expenses can be reduced, or eliminated. It could be your daily trips to your favorite coffee shop, or cable tv that you do not really use, or a regular manicure/pedicure. You will be amazed at how much you can save when you consistently review your expenses, and improve on your spending habits.

4. **Make extra income or increase your income**

    This is not hard to do, if you take an inventory of what you can do or improve. This can challenge your skills and creativity. When I divorced 10 years ago, I suddenly lost a big source of income as my husband's income was almost twice as much as my income. I had to replace his income. I established lines of credit in order to get my basement redone, so that I would have two bedrooms to rent out. I make $1,100.00 every month. I started to loan out money, and made interest income. I bought cheaper US real estate and make rental income in US funds. During tax seasons, I was preparing tax returns for friends and family. I had converted a very financially stressful situation into a less stressful situation, and later on, a comfortable situation.

5. **List your regular expenses**

    If you list your regular expenses, and write down the amounts you are spending, you will see how much you are spending, and you can evaluate which expenses can be cut or reduced. Separate needs from wants. Needs are musts, and hard to be removed, while wants are always dispensable things that you can easily decide to let go. Expenses can be categorized into fixed, flexible and discretionary.

Fixed expenses- regular amounts that generally don't change much. Examples are mortgage, rent, car payments, car registration and insurance.

Flexible expenses – are necessities. We buy regularly, but we have more control over how much we spend. Examples are groceries and cellphone bills.

Discretionary expenses- these are what we choose to spend money on, such as clothes, movies, vacations and going out to eat.

6. **Stop using or control using your credit cards**
   When you are not putting out immediate cash because you are using a credit card, it is very easy for you to make a buying decision. Then we get shocked at payment time when we see how much we have to pay on our credit cards. Many people get trapped in credit card debts, and due to the ever increasing debts, they are left with no choice but to pay the minimum amounts, and have to pay for the rest of their lives with high interest. When you are using cash instead of credit card, you will think twice or thrice before you make a purchase.

7. **Save up for purchases instead of putting them on credit**
   Most people will use credit cards for large purchases they can not afford to pay outright, like vacations or a new appliance or furniture. What I do, is I set aside money coming either from an additional income I made or savings I made for cutting on some expenses. Again, this is part of budgeting and planning that we should learn and train ourselves in. If we can not afford to save up for the purchase, then we can not afford to buy what we want.

8. **Have an emergency fund**
   If you have savings dedicated only for emergencies, then you do not have to resort to using credit cards. You can have

emergency fund equivalent to three or six months of living expenses, or whatever is comfortable for you. This will give you the habit of saving and setting aside funds for any purpose other than emergency. People in a real emergency situation can resort to other ways of raising the money other than using credit cards, like selling their valuables at much lower proceeds.

9.   Do not live up to the Joneses
Nowadays, people tend to be always up to date in fashion, technology and life's pleasures and luxuries. Our human tendency is to have the same material things and pleasures. You may be able to use your credit cards and lines of credits to afford them, but you will pay for it later. In most cases, you will end up paying more or could be in financial trouble. If we continue to compare ourselves with others, it will rob us of happiness and leave us in debt. As Mark Twain said " Comparison is the death of joy."

10.   Check your credit score/beacon rating
This is a good opportunity to check your credit score. You can get your credit score from either Equifax or Transunion. A good credit score will give you access to lower interest rates and therefore easier to get credits or loans, when you have to borrow. Generally, you need a good credit to get cash-back and other types of reward credit cards that will help you get maximum value for your spending. If you have good credit, the banks and lending institutions will be chasing you because you are a good credit risk to them. You can use it to your advantage since when you are in business, you definitely need it. I use my excellent credit score in opening lines of credits for my real estate investments.

11. Make the change/manage your money better

If you find yourself constantly short of funds and relying on credit cards or loans to make up the difference, this means you are living beyond your means. This may require you to make some major changes to your lifestyle and spending habits. Looking at and streamlining your budget can help you have an idea of where you stand financially and help you set goals to where you want to be. Focus on paying down debts, and saving money for the future instead of spending mindlessly.

12. Have an attitude of gratitude

Much overspending could be avoided if we appreciate what we already have. Oftentimes, we buy things because we are feeling bored, lonely or upset. What can we do? The next time we feel like indulging or shopping, make a list of ten things we are grateful for first. Switching your focus from what you do not have to what you already have puts finances in their proper perspective. Accumulating stuff cannot bring long-term happiness, only a long-term misery.

13. Pay your bills on time

Have a good control and discipline of paying your bills on time. This will help you to avoid being charged hefty interests and penalties, losing possession or being evicted for non-payment of rent. This will also keep your credit score high. It will avoid stressful situations and keep you out of money troubles. It will keep you always mindful of your budget, and you will conscientiously negotiate for better terms with service providers and suppliers and keep you in control of your expenses.

14. Reward yourself

I reward myself after meeting my savings goal, or successfully meeting my income and expenses budgets. This will motivate me to work harder and better. This will also encourage me to have more ideas, to make more money and be more spending conscious, so I can make more real estate ventures and investments.

15. Always stop and know needs and wants
Before each and every purchase, ask yourself " Do I really need this?" If the answer is no, then drop that item, because you do not need it.

16. Look at the future
Many people spend like there is no tomorrow. No matter how uncomfortable, we should ask questions like, "How will I have my house paid earlier?", or "What legacy will I leave to my children?" or "How can I retire comfortably?"

17. Do not buy because it is on sale
Many of us become victims of buying products because they are on sale. Make this to your advantage, if you truly need the product or service that is on sale. But, if you are buying because it is cheaper than before, and you want to take advantage of it, you are stocking up on an item that you most likely do not need, and will eventually get rid of it, or never use. In the meantime, you will be indebted, and if you are buying on credit, you are adding interest that can take you forever to pay.

18. Find alternative activities
Many of us get hooked on impulsive buying, or emotional shopping, because we do not have anything better to do. Or, we use it as a form of entertainment. Find alternative activities that are inexpensive, or even free. Why not walk, or enroll in a gym membership? Or, borrow a book from the library. Call, or see a friend, who is not a spender. Develop a new hobby.

19. Make trade-offs

If we can not afford everything we want to buy, we can make a trade-off. It means giving up something for another thing that is more important or valuable to you now. Let us say, for example, I trade off going to the beauty parlor for a manicure and pedicure so I can go to the gym for workouts, and be more fit and lose weight.

20. Stop or reduce your trips to the stores

If you do not have to go to the store or to the mall, do not go. If you do not want to use your credit card, or your hard earned cash, do not go. You will prevent yourself from drowning in debt for unnecessary things. Time is so valuable; you will find out, if you seriously look for better things to do with your time. Finding a way to make money, or do something good for yourself or for someone else is worth a lot more than a trip to the store.

Frugality can be a virtue, and living within your means is a way of staying out of financial trouble.

CHAPTER 8
READ, READ, READ

"We need books, time and silence. Once upon a time lasts forever."

I have been reading all my life starting at age seven and a half with my first book being *Pepe and Pilar*. I started schooling in grade one and as I was growing up in my adolescent years, I developed the habit of reading. I enjoyed the stories about legends, stories, history and science, and just about anything else. I got curious about how much there was to learn and discover in the world. I was hungry for knowledge, and as I have a deep ambition to get out of poverty and improve my life, reading became a habit.

In my university years, in the oldest university in Asia, University of SantoTomas, there were libraries that I truly enjoyed. At the College of Commerce where I majored in Entrepreneurship, I would be at the library after my classes. Since we could not afford to buy textbooks or other books during those times, I used the library a lot, to my advantage.

I borrowed books, and researched to complete my assignments and projects. Reading brought me to writing. It seems like reading and writing are twins. I loved writing so much that I became the Section Editor of the Entrepreneurship Major. I was given a stipend for every article I wrote. I wrote my thesis, and read and read about my subject.

Thesis writing was a requirement. So, I went to the bigger library of the university, at the main building, the Humanities Library. I got a grade of 97% for writing that thesis with revalida. All thesis with a grade of 95% and higher, are donated to the university to be used by students. I could not be happier, at that time, for being able to donate something from my hard work and labor. During those times, there was no computer or Microsoft Word. I was typing those pages of thesis on a borrowed typewriter. I remember typing up to two in the morning even though I had to wake up at five am to go to school for seven am class. I was having fun, and I was driven by my strong desire to always do my very best.

When I graduated from the university, I pursued to study one more major -Accountancy. Then, I took the CPA Board Exams. Studying forces me to read and read and the routine of reading led me to more reading. Then, I started to read pocketbooks. In my later years, when I went to business and real estate, I was reading business and real estate books. Then, as life has its ups and downs, I started to read motivational and inspirational books. According to Warren Buffet, one of the most successful people in the business world, the art of reading is his best kept secret to success. Knowledge becomes power.

We have been taught, from a very young age that reading as much as possible is the pathway to success and fulfillment. While being an avid reader does not ensure success, successful people surely are avid readers.

Books are full of magic and mystery, and reading should be a joy, not an obligation. I mean to encourage all readers to read everyday and all the time. Happy and successful people read at least one book every week. And, here is why we should read whether it be books, magazines, audio books or from the internet.

1. **For pleasure and enjoyment**
    Real life stories and fiction alike, entertains us. Reading brings us to the fantasy lands, fairy tales bring us tears and laughter, and real life stories give us real life lessons. There are reading genres for everyone, whether your interest is literature, poetry, self-help guides, romance novels, etc. It is found that reading improves one's life, and helps one to feel good, and thereby become happier.

2. **Stimulates the mind**
    Reading stimulates the mind, and can slow or prevent Alzheimer's and Dementia. Keeping the brain active prevents it from losing power. The brain requires exercise to keep it strong and healthy. As the saying goes, "use it or lose it".

3. **Makes you a better writer**
    When you read vigorously, it fills your mind and soul. As you are filled with knowledge and vocabularies, it makes you a better writer. Your brain translates to your hand in writing all that you know, and all that you want to share to your readers and to the world. The more you read, the better writer you will become.

4. **Reduces Stress**
    We always have stress at work, in our personal relationships, and other areas of our lives. Whatever they are, they just slip away when we bury our face in a great story or novel, or inspirational book. It makes us relax, and keeps us in the present moment, rather than worrying about something.

5. **Gain knowledge**
    As we read, we stack a lot of knowledge in our head. We discover new things. We live in an age of overflowing information, and reading is the main way of getting to know

it. The more knowledge we have, the better person we become - equipped and ready with all that we have learned, when we are faced with a challenge. And as my mother always said to me when I was young, "Get an education and fill your mind with knowledge", it is all yours for the taking. I can lose everything – money, possessions, my job, but knowledge is all mine, and can not be taken away from me.

6. **Expands vocabulary**
    When you read, you increase your vocabulary. I remember when I was reading, and the books would have difficult words to understand, I would have a dictionary side by side with the book I was reading. Because of this, I also became good at spelling. I became a spelling bee candidate in high school. Also, when you learn new words and become better with your vocabulary, it is easier to play around with your sentences, and easier to write. And when we write well, it works to our advantage. As it is said, "The pen is mightier than the sword."

7. **Boosts self-esteem and confidence**
    To become knowledgeable, articulate and well-spoken can be a great help in your work, profession or business. It allows you to speak with comfort and boosts your self-esteem. It also builds your self-confidence as you obtain knowledge and information that you know, but many people do not know. The feeling of having this advantage makes you feel good and builds self-confidence.

8. **Improves memory**
    When you read a book, you tend to remember events, characters, dates, history and other important details. This helps to improve our memory, as we exercise our brain when we try to remember them.

9. **Makes better analytical skills**

   When we read, and there are problems involved with what we are reading, it makes us adopt an analytical skill before finishing the book. The ability to analyze comes in handy when we are faced with situations requiring it. If we are given an opportunity to discuss the book we have read with others, we are able to state our opinions clearly, as we have taken the time to consider all the aspects involved.

10. **Improves focus and concentration**

    When we read a book, all our attention is focused on the story – our world stops for a moment as we are fully engrossed in every detail that we are absorbing.

11. **Peace and tranquility**

    If we are reading inspirational or spiritual texts in a book, it brings about an immense sense of calmness, peace and tranquility. It can lower our blood pressure. It helps us have better attitudes, and improve our bad moods.

12. **Helps you sleep better**

    Reading creates a relaxed disengagement that helps induce a perfect environment for helping you sleep. Especially for those with insomnia, the last activity of the day disengages you from the tasks of the rest of the day.

13. **Helps prioritize goals**

    Reading gives our minds a chance to wander. When we remove ourselves from our work environment, we start to see things that we might really want to do, that we are not doing yet. Reading can show us the things we did not know about ourselves. It is the reading that can push us into what we really want to do.

How To Read More

So, now you are convinced that you should read, but you say, you do not have time to read. How can I read more? Sitting down to read does not mean you have to carve an hour or more out of your day. There are many ways you can sneak more reading into your life. Here are some suggestions.

1. **Watch less TV**
   This is a very easy way to get more time to read. You can read in the morning before starting work, or in the evening after work or before going to sleep. When you get used to it, then it becomes a very good habit, just like brushing your teeth. And you will not be missing your TV anymore.

2. **Use less internet**
   Many of us become addicted and hooked on internet, especially social media. We do not notice how much time we are using everyday on the internet. We can easily replace reading with internet trawling.

3. **Invest in tablet device**
   It was found out that those who own a tablet, or e-reader spend more time reading than they used to. You can download books for free. This is a very easy and cheap way to get quick and portable access to the world's best books. You can take your entire library with you on a plane, train, or in your purse. You can read while waiting at the doctor's or dentist's office, or while you're in line at the grocery store.

4. **Listen to audiobooks and podcasts**
   This is twice the speed than when you are reading it. There is speed reading and smart reading, nowadays, that can cut your audio listening in half, and will allow you to listen more, and gain more knowledge and enjoyment.

5. Choose the right books that interest you

It is not because a book is popular and everybody is talking about it, that you should read it. Find out what really interests you. If you start with these kinds of books, then you will get more pleasure and value out of the experience.

6. Set a time

You need to pick a time that will suit your own schedule. Even if it is only 10-15 minutes a day, it is still a good way to develop the habit, help you relax, and allow you to momentarily forget about the stresses of everyday life, in a healthy way. I can read in the morning after my prayers and affirmations, for a few minutes, or at night after dinner, until before going to bed.

7. Read with others

Reading with your kids is a wonderful way to teach them the love of reading. But reading with others, such as with friends or as part of a book club, can also be a rewarding and motivating way to read more. There are also online book clubs you can join. These clubs expose you to books you might not have heard about, and they also give you the opportunity to discuss what you have read and learned with others.

8. Find a time during your spare times

There is plenty of time to bury yourself in books or an e-reader. This is a good time to evaluate how we are making use of our free time. How about your break times at work or waiting for an appointment - reduce shopping time, or reduce entertainment time (and save some money, too).

Books For Success

Here are my recommendations for must-read books for success. These are the books most read, liked and have made a difference in many lives. These books take a comprehensive approach to life, money and personal development.

1. ***Think and Grow Rich*** by Napoleon Hill
   Written by Napoleon Hill and inspired by business legend Andrew Carnegie, he spent 20 years of his life studying the lives of some of the history's most successful people. The culmination of his research resulted in an in-depth series, The Laws of Success. In 1937, Napoleon Hill published the book, *Think and Grow Rich*, founded on the same philosophies of success. This book condensed the wealth of knowledge he had accumulated into 13 principles for successful living.

2. ***The Law of Success In Sixteen Lessons*** by Napoleon Hill
   Twenty years of research, including interviews with more than 500 self-made millionaires, laid the foundation for this massive collection. After studying the methods and accomplishments of masterminds such as Thomas Edison, John Rockefeller, Henry Ford, Andrew Carnegie, Theodore Roosevelt and Alexander Graham Bell. Napoleon Hill compiled what he learned, offering it to the world as the Laws of Success.

3. ***Rich Dad Poor Dad*** by Robert T. Kiyosaki
   The paradigm shift related to work, employment and entrepreneurship, has been a long time coming. In one of his most-read books, *Rich Dad Poor Dad*, Robert Kiyosaki reveals the value of taking control of your finances through entrepreneurship and investing. In *Rich Dad Poor Dad*, Kiyosaki contrasts the differences between the rich and the

poor or middle classes, in how they teach their children. As a young man, Kiyosaki was taught by his 'poor dad' to follow the path of least resistance - get an education, get a job and work hard. His 'rich dad' , his friend's dad, mentored him in the opposite way. The book acknowledges that education is important but isn't always best received in a formal learning environment. Lessons include the value of self-employment, how to be self-employed without limiting yourself to the constraints of an employee, and how to create and take advantage of residual-income opportunities. Instead of working hard for the money, use the principles in this book to make money for you.

4. *Who Moved My Cheese* by Dr. Spencer Johnson
For many people, change can be challenging. It can cause fear, anger and the feeling of being out of control. This popular parable examines change and what happens to those who choose not to embrace it. 'If you do not change, you can become extinct', is one of the many truisms the characters learn in *Who Moved My Cheese?* In the maze of life, it is possible to successfully deal with change, if and when, you clear your mind of expectations and understand that while your comfort zone may be cozy, it is not necessarily the safest place to live.

**For a complete list of success books, go to
www.journeytoanewyou.com.**

CHAPTER 9
AN ATTITUDE OF GRATITUDE

"Be thankful for what you have; you'll end up having more.
If you concentrate on what you don't have, you will never,
ever have enough."

When I was young, I did not know what gratitude was all about. All I had was the 'lack of all'. Lack of money, lack of comforts, lack of a nice place to live, lack of I thought was everything I could dream of.

I did not appreciate the beauty and blessings of what I had – my very good parents, my three pious and hardworking sisters, my four protective brothers, close relatives surrounding us where we lived, and all their love. I even failed to see the joy that I was brought forth to in this world with so much bright future waiting…

All I did then was complain and ask.

When I asked, and worked hard for it, then I learned to say thank you. When in danger and got I through it, I said thank you. And, it became a habit, and life became so much more glorious…

And, as I journeyed through life, I discovered that there were so many blessings to count and so much to be thankful for, and that gratitude is much more than being thankful and grateful. It is an acknowledgement, and feeling the presence of God and who we are grateful for. As long as we are grateful for anything and everything, we have more peace and happiness. It attracts more, and give you more of what you are grateful for.

Gratitude means thankfulness, counting your blessings, noticing simple pleasures, and acknowledging everything that you receive. It means learning to live your life as if everything is a miracle, and being aware on a continuous basis of how much you have been given. Gratitude shifts your focus from what your life lacks to the abundance that is already present. In addition, behavioral and psychological research has shown the surprising life improvements that can stem from the practice of gratitude. Giving thanks makes people happier and more resilient, it strengthens relationships, it improves health, and it reduces stress.

It seems that humans are hardwired to see the negative in life, and focus on them, and envy other people and become miserable. When I got divorced in 2006, I suddenly reframed my thinking into believing that being alone as a single parent with four growing up children was hard and lonely. But, with courage and fortitude, I stood firmer and stronger, and decided I have all the time and opportunity to cultivate and do more, now that I am on my own and independent. I formed new relationships with same-minded people in the areas of success and slowly, I became happier and happier, and had more intent and purpose in life. I developed the daily habit of gratitude, and life to me has never been more enriching and fulfilling. I started to write in my gratitude journals, and say my positive affirmations. This works like miracles! The more I kept saying what I was thankful for, the more I had of them! I gave thanks for having a mentor for the first time in my life. Then I had one more, and then another one. I gave thanks for my first European trip; then I had another within the same year, and another one the following year! If we still do not believe in the law of attraction and the power of the subconscious mind, I do not know what else to call it.

The benefits of gratitude can be life-changing. When we are constantly being grateful, we can achieve the following:

1. Gratitude puts a situation in perspective. When we can see the good as well as the bad, it becomes more difficult to complain and stay stuck.

2. Gratitude helps us realize what we have. This can lessen our need for wanting more all the time.

3. Gratitude strengthens relationships, improves health, reduces stress, and in general, makes us happier.

4. Gratitude increases our sense of well-being, awareness, enthusiasm, happiness, determination and optimism.

5. Gratitude raises our vibrational frequency, and creates an upward-spiraling process of ever increasing joy and abundance, that just keeps getting better and better.

How Can We Cultivate Gratitude

1. Notice our day-to-day world from a point of view of gratitude and be amazed at all the goodness we take for granted. I thank my daughter's dog for giving me so much joy and pleasure. I thank for my other daughter for giving me my grandson Leon, who is so smart and loveable, life would not be this happy and exciting without him.

2. Keep a gratitude journal. I note five new things I am grateful for, each and every day. I do this at night and I sleep in joy and peace for all five items I highlighted for that day. You

can choose a time of day when you have several minutes to reflect and thankfully write them down. Freshen up your thanks by having new, specific or different reasons for your gratitude. As your write them down in your journal, really feel the appreciation and give thanks. This time spent in gratitude will become a sacred part of your daily routine. Be grateful for even the difficult and challenging situations in your life. These situations contribute to your spiritual and emotional growth. Often, they are opportunities to develop a new quality, strength, skill, insight or wisdom. Be grateful for the lessons and growth they provide.

3. If we identify something or someone with a negative trait, switch it in your mind to a positive trait. I used to be so impatient with people who are slow, and now I say, yes he is slow, because he is thorough and careful.

4. Give at least one compliment daily. It can be given to a person or you can ask someone to share your appreciation of something else.

5. When you find yourself in a bad situation ask: What can I learn? What will I be grateful for? When I am driving and get lost, I used to fret about losing time and wasting gas. But then, I say to myself, I discovered a new place, and now it adds up to my stock of knowledge about places.

6. Vow not to complain, criticize, or gossip for a day. If you slip, fight back and keep going. Notice the amount of energy you were spending on negative thoughts and actions. You can shift to doing things that are worth more your time and look at the positive side of people and events, rather than attracting negative vibes from complaining, criticizing and gossiping. These are damaging, and may give you troubles.

7. Sound genuinely happy to hear from the people who call you on the phone. Whether the caller responds with surprise or delight, he'll know you value speaking with him.

8. Become involved in a cause that is important to you. Donate money or talent. By joining in, you will gain greater appreciation for the organization, and it will appreciate you more, too.

How Can We Show Gratitude

1. **Say thank you all the time**
   It is the best prayer that anyone could say. Say that a lot, and all the time. Thank you expresses extreme gratitude, humility and understanding. It makes us feel good acknowledging our appreciation, and the receiver also feels good about our appreciation of what they did for us. The more we thank, the more we get things done for us.

2. **Count your blessings**
   You will be surprised how much you have, and how fast you will forget what you do not have. There is a saying *I was complaining I have no new shoes, until I saw somebody without feet.* List all the things you have that you should be thankful for and you will be amazed at how much you have; you will have no need to look for more.

3. **See the positive in the negative.**
   I used to fret and get upset when something bad happened to me, or when I make a mistake. Then I started seeing the positive, and the lesson, even from the worst event or mistake; it just made me better and happier.

4. **Verbally say thank you instead of by email or text.**
   Saying thank you in person, whenever possible, is always

much more appreciated than when you say it in a text message or email. Direct contact, where you can show your facial expression, and use a good tone of voice, or even give a handshake or a hug, is always a better way to express gratitude.

5. Write thank you notes and cards.
Most people nowadays will quickly send an email or a text to say thank you. The old fashioned way of sending a thank you note, or a card is still very powerful, as the recipient appreciates your time and effort, not only in getting the card, but also for writing the thank you note in your own handwriting, getting a stamp, and mailing it.

Express gratitude, not only for the good things that you receive, but also for the challenges, problems and bad events that happen to you. These teach you great lessons in life, and helps you know how to deal with them, and as we get better in handling them, the happier and more successful we become.

CHAPTER 10
GET IT DONE

*"You may delay, but time will not,
and lost time is never found again."*

From my humble beginnings, I was trained to do a lot of things, as times were hard.

I did all kinds of household chores, such as cleaning the house, doing errands for my mother, helping my mother or sister with the cooking in the kitchen, washing dishes, feeding the chickens, washing clothes, drying clothes, and ironing clothes. You name it, I have done it. At age nine, I started working by helping my sister sell fish in the market. I used to wake up at two in the morning to go with my sister to the fish port to get the fish and bring them to the market. I was not bothered by the fish smell, or all the hardships. After selling fish for about half a day, my sister would have money and would take me to a restaurant to eat, buy a quarter kilo of chestnuts (it was expensive for us, so could not afford a kilo), or even took me to the movies. I saw that if you worked hard, you would get money, and you could buy what you want and afford something. At age thirteen, my other sister put up a small garments factory at our house. From selling fish, I went to sewing baby dresses for my sister. I also did all the other stuff-hemming clothes, sorting clothes, cutting, buying materials, selling the dresses in the market. And at the same time, I had to study. I had to work to make money, while studying at the same time, so that I could help my parents and sisters support my studying.

Poverty with ambition and a very strong desire for a better life, propelled me to get things done no matter what and whatever it would take.

I am not just sharing this story for the people who have the same kind of life as I had. Today, many of you are very blessed because you are not in poverty, you have more technology, you have more resources to learn from, there are more available credits for capital, and you can get your mentor to expedite your success and happiness. All you need is you – your desire, your discipline and the willingness - to just do it!

Remember that we have goals in life that we want to achieve, and if we are not in control of how we can get things done, then we are in trouble of not accomplishing our goals.

So we must start with great habits, to get things done. Never do tomorrow what you can do today. Procrastination is the thief of time. I had a formal training in *Louis Allen Management and Leadership Principles* during my Union Carbide career. I want to share this with you because these principles worked very well for me in my working life, my business life and in my personal life as well. With *Louis Allen* in my systems, I learned if I am a better manager, I have better results.

1. **To-Do List**
   Creating a to-do list is part of planning. I learned this during my early working life in the 1980's, and while this may be old-fashioned, it still is an effective way of planning. List everything that you have to do in a day. Put time lines on every task. You can re-evaluate your list and rank by priority so you can focus on the more important and urgent ones. Then you check them off, one by one. You can keep a notebook, and you can write your notes as your day goes along.

2. Set deadlines

Analyze every activity or task, and assign how much time is needed to complete it. Time is of the essence. We do not have all the time in the world, as the saying goes. Efficiency is a trait that is a must, in all facets of our life. I have learned that when I budget time for what I have to do, I am in control and surely to get it done. Without assigned time, you are floating into the world of 'anything can happen'. And, you end up doing the things you want to do, and not what you have to do.

3. Avoid distractions

It is very easy to have distractions that can derail your to-do lists, and will make the list take longer to finish, get postponed or not done at all. Turn off your cellphone, shut off your computer, turn off the TV or radio and stop wasting time talking endlessly. There is a time for everything. When you have no distractions, you can focus and you have a better chance of speedily getting your task done with the highest quality possible.

4. Focus on one activity at a time

We can have several things to do, and we can get tangled up with all of them if we do not know how to handle them. We can multitask, but do not sacrifice quality. Starting at so many tasks and not finishing all of them, and leaving them hanging in the air will also not get you anywhere. I concentrate and put all my heart into one activity at a time. When you finish a task and get it done, you move on to the next. Get it done. Move to the next. What a great feeling, and it boosts your energy at a higher level. And by the law of attraction, you are just doing all that you want to accomplish.

5. **Start from easy to hard**
   You may want to start with the easy tasks that take only a few minutes to do. For example, taking out garbage does take only two minutes, while a project will take you a few hours.

6. **Prioritize**
   We can be swarmed at certain points in our lives, even if we have done all the planning, as some things can come unexpectedly. We should prioritize and exercise best judgment. Do things that are most important and urgent. Some things have to be done first, some things can be done second and some things can be done last.

7. **Organize**
   In *Louie Allen Management Principles*, organizing is the second. It is the process of identifying and grouping works to be performed, defining and delegating responsibility and authority, and establishing relationships for the purpose of enabling people to work efficiently. As we say, "Don't agonize. Organize". Organizing helps you to specialize, and have more effective, well- coordinated tasks, and optimizes utilization of resources. In my job as an Accountant, Realtor, Real Estate Investor and Coach, I have learned to be organized in my paperwork and documents, and to make sure that I do not miss any task. I have become more efficient and very fast in doing things, to avoid the impact of not doing things on time. Organizing reduces stress, and we are more confident that things are getting done well, and on time.

8. **Control**
   It is determining what is being accomplished, and if necessary, applying corrective actions. It is when you check the work from the beginning to the end of the task. This can

apply whether you are doing it yourself or you delegate the job to somebody else. When a task is checked, whether you are the one checking, or your job is the one being checked, you are sure you are on track and doing it correctly. It is a waste of time, very frustrating and can be damaging when you spent so much time and effort, just to find out afterwards that it was not what you were supposed to do.

9. **Communicate**

Doing something can require communication to get it done. Communicating allows to make clear goals and objectives. It can help define our expectations to ensure it is done properly and on time. If we communicate effectively, we avoid misunderstanding and conflict. We avoid paying for mistakes at a high cost. To effectively communicate, we have to do it promptly and at the right time. We can communicate face to face, by email, by letter, or text. We do not simply ask, we ask questions and we clarify. We are honest and sincere. And we persuade and negotiate if we have to.

10. **Coordinate**

This is essential to channel the activities of various individuals working to achieve the common goal. This is when we ensure that are activities are aligned to everybody else. There is no duplication of work, and everybody is doing his specific duties.

CHAPTER 11
INVEST IN YOURSELF

"To invest in yourself is the best investment of all"

We know of all kinds of investments – real estate, stocks, bonds, gold, jewelries. And there is one investment that is the best investment, that is almost always overlooked. And this is the only guaranteed investment in life.

And that's you. Yes, that's you. You are your own greatest asset.

When I first heard this phrase, I did not pay attention, and I thought it was strange. I have always been busy dealing with life, struggling and working. When I got married, I had four children, so life was pretty hectic. I put all my energy and investment in my family and children. I was not a priority.

Then I would get sick at times, even hospitalized, and then I would realize that I should invest in myself health-wise. I have young kids who rely on me. Then, at some points, we lose jobs and have to find alternate ways of making a living. Then, I learned, I should have other skills and a fallback position. So, then I realized I should study real estate and get a license, and I could do it at on my own time so that I could still look after my children. And, that real estate license gave me more independence and financial freedom. That real estate license that I earned after only three months of studying after putting my kids to sleep, gave me a lifetime advantage over an ordinary woman my age. I was making more income than my husband, with less working hours. I got exposures to the outside world of the rich and famous, as they became my clients. I would not have been able to do that if I was at the confines of a regular '9-5' office job like what I used to be.

Investing in ourselves in both personal and professional growth, consistently throughout our lifetime, plays a large role in determining the quality of our life.

What I discovered is that when we invest in ourselves, it opens the world of opportunities. Investing in ourselves emotionally, physically, spiritually and financially will allow us to become a better version of ourselves. When we become better, we can easily be a magnet to others, and will attract happiness and success.

What are the ways we can invest in ourselves?

1. **Advance your education**
   Take extra classes, advanced degrees, get relevant certifications or diplomas. You can do it in person or online. Take no excuses that you do not have time. I got my license when I had two kids and had just recently given birth to my youngest child. Make no excuses that you do not have money. There are government supports, scholarships and bursaries. There are available bank lines of credits, credit cards, or even family support. If there is a will, there is a way. I finished my university degree , and my parents had no regular income. You will be amazed at how solutions to problems just happen when you have a strong will and determination.

2. **Invest in new skills**

   Your education doesn't have to stop at high school, college or university. Not only does learning a new skill help you keep your resume fresh, but it can help you discover new passions and interests in life. Take advantage of professional development opportunities at your current job or take a class in a creative field you're interested in, like painting or writing. You may be surprised what you learn and where your new skill set takes you.

3. **Utilize available training**

   There are so many workshops, seminars, boot camps, meet ups and conferences. Many are free, and some have only a nominal fee. Some are in webinars, some you should do in person. You can be working '8-5' Monday to Friday, but there is training available after work hours or on week-ends. They are very valuable in getting information, ideas and networking opportunities. Choose the area or subject that you are interested in. If I do not know where to find available training, I just google and call and find out. When you start with one and try the others for comparison, then it will open you up to all other training opportunities, like a wild fire in the forest. You will now be choosing which group, or which way to go. You will meet and interact with like-minded people.

4. **Expand your knowledge**

   There are lots of information on any subject of your choice. Make use of the library to read books, and articles. You can also use the internet and use it to your advantage. Keep current, and abreast, with the latest trends or advancements and follow the latest news on your interests.

5. **Develop a new skill or hobby**

   You can explore your creative side and potential. If we tap into it, it can help us grow personally and professionally. We can try new things like writing a book or articles in our areas of interest or specialization. As I was travelling, I developed the hobby of photography, as I did not want to miss the beautiful sceneries, locations and moments of my travels. This gives me so much happiness and lifetime memories and encourages me to travel more and improve my photo-taking skills. I even took a two-hour course in photography.

6. **Enjoy music**

   You can learn to play a musical instrument, join a music group, or simply enjoy listening to it. I have no particular inclination to learning any musical instrument, but I had CD's, DVD's, spotify, xirius xm, music selections in my laptop, iPad and iPhone as music gives me an unexplainable joy and entertainment in what could be a boring or busy life.

7. **Invest in your health**

   Being healthy is the best way to insure your other investments in life keep up. Investing in your health can be as simple as a having a healthy breakfast each morning. It could mean drinking at least 8 glasses of water everyday. It could mean walking 30 minutes everyday. It could mean eating fresh fruits and vegetables instead of junk foods. It could mean having enough sleep and rest. I never fail to go to my doctor at least once a year and dentist twice a year for a regular check-up. Do something daily to invest in your health and you'll be sure that you will be able to take care of your family, and be productive at work. Then it will surely make you, and the people you love be happy, too.

8. Invest in your spiritual life

"For without me, you can do nothing." I used to think and act like I didn't need an 'almighty' to fulfill my dreams and do what I want to do. Then, I was shown the way, that I needed not only my 'mighty', but the 'almighty' who created me, and to whom I owe everything. I reflected and re-established a relationship with my Creator, and life had been good once again. This is the biggest lesson of my life – that you put God first in your life and have your relationship with Him be your first priority. I wake up in joy, and sleep in peace, with God in me. And my day just flows smoothly and if there are issues, they are easily handled and solved. I still believe in going to my church every Saturday afternoon, praying after waking up, praying before sleeping and talking to God as often as possible. I now thank God more often than any other time in my life. It is incredible that I mention God so many times in a day as there are countless blessings and opportunities, whether good or challenging. And God never abandons me. He is always there. If you have a constant, strong relationship with God, everything else that is good follows. You will experience the fullness of God's blessings, and He is so good all the time.

9. Invest In Your Exterior Looks

As we take care of our emotional, physical and mental states, let us not forget our exterior looks, or simply how we look. We need this as we are social beings, and we meet and interact everyday. We have to make good impressions that happen in the first two seconds that people look at us. So it's better that we make it good and lasting. Wearing nice, clean, and decent clothes, makes us feel good about ourselves, and truly boosts our well-being and self-confidence. It forms part of our personality and character, with which other people would like to thrive with.

10. Get a mentor

This may not be for everyone as our goals are all different and our levels of growth and dreams are in different stages. I did not believe in a mentor all my life until just a few years ago, when I decided I needed one. I decided to go to the next level and created new goals that would require a mentor in the field of real estate and success. And where do you find a mentor when you have decided that you need one? "When the student is ready, the teacher will appear" as the saying goes. In my case, as I was talking with the Broker of Record of my real estate brokerage, that was how I found my mentor. The mentor is somebody who has gone successfully to climb Mt. Everest. So if climbing Mt. Everest is your goal, then get somebody who has done it.

With a mentor, you are more guaranteed to succeed with your goal in the shortest time, less effort and probably less costlier than if you would do it on your own or with somebody who has no proven track record. The mentor can cost you money, but the likelihood of success of meeting that goal is higher, and the cost of the mentor could be a drop in the bucket compared to the benefits you get. The mentors usually give a 30 minute complimentary meeting so you can assess whether that mentor resonates with your goals and objectives, before hiring him. Where to find a mentor best for you? Start with google, or ask people you know, or if they can think of someone. You will surely find one.

11. Heal from your hurts and pains

I used to cry a lot or fret about hurts and pains. It was very demeaning and humiliating. It could be disastrous, and prevents us to moving on with life, and makes us think life is not fair. We are vulnerable to many happenings and events in our lives. We experience death of loved ones, separations, divorces, lost relationships, job losses, business losses - anything that offends our feelings and emotions. I have been through all these. But I rose up, learned from them and became a better person. The other habits that I have talked about in this book can help. You exercise, you develop some new hobbies, go places, meet people. You can also seek professional help, if needed. In time, we all heal, and it is as though the hurts and pains never happened.

CHAPTER 12
NURTURE RELATIONSHIPS

"Nurture a healthy relationship with every aspect of your humanity and you will find endless possibilities, creative solutions and moments exceeding all expectations"

As human beings, we all need love and support from our relationships. This is basic to a happy and successful life. We are social creatures who crave friendship and positive interactions. The better our relationships, the happier and more productive we are going to be.

My loving relationship started with my family-my parents, my three sisters and my four brothers. Then I had grandparents, uncles and aunts, brothers-in-law, sisters-in-law, cousins, nephews and nieces and all the extended families. Then I had my own family – my husband and four children. Then from work, I had bosses, officemates and friends. Then, I had a business and I had clients and suppliers. And, so on and so forth. We all have relationships, in all forms. We are not alone, and we have needs, and have to work with others to be happy and successful. In many careers and businesses, the success revolves around and lies, mainly on relationships. It is all about relationships.

So, let us talk about relationships, since it is critical.

Why Have Good Relationships?

1. Our life becomes more enjoyable when we have good relationships with those we love and care about. Family is the basic unit of society; a happy family creates a happy and productive society.

2. We need the support of family, friends, associates, and business associates to help each other in moral, financial, physical or emotional areas. If we have great relationships, we have better support that makes us happier and more successful.

3. In the workplace, workers become one family as they work together and spend more hours together than their biological family. People are more likely to go along with changes, or what we want to implement. If we get along well with everyone, it is easier to get their cooperation with changes, and the demands of our work are met. In management, line managers and supervisors are trained to better handle their subordinates and get their loyalty, dedication and continuous improvement for work.

4. Poor relationships cause stress, anxiety and worse, depression. The happier is the relationship, the less stress and less anxiety, and the healthier we are.

5. Great relationships boost our well-being and self-esteem. This contributes toward greater motivation to work, higher achievement and success.

How Do We Keep Healthy Relationships?

Communicate
This is key to building a healthy relationship. We make sure we are on the same page. We make sure we want the same thing and expect the same thing. We have to be open and talk about something that is bothering us as opposed to holding it in. We respect others wishes and feelings. The ability to communicate, or not, can spell the difference between success and failure. We can agree to disagree, and arrive at a compromise. We build each other up, instead of putting each other down.

Spend time together
We need to boost or re-bond with people we care about if we feel disconnected. Find a way to see each other and have fun together. It can be as simple as walking together, having coffee, watching a movie, or anything that you both like and enjoy. This gives us an opportunity to share what is currently going on in our lives, and share ideas on anything. This gives us so much joy and contentment when we are able to rejuvenate any stale relationship.

Attend reunions
I love attending reunions, whether family reunions, class reunions or office reunions. When you have built solid relationships in any area, and then you are apart, as life leads us to different ways, reunions are a good way to reconnect with more people during one event, after many years. We relive our past and memories just never die. And when we reunite, we add more everlasting memories. Old relationships are proven and tested, and we can always rely on old friends to be loyal and be on our side.

Make new friends/Network
Nowadays, it is easier and faster to make more friends. We have all forms of social media where we can make friends in an instant, and grow from there. I have made so many friends on Facebook and Instagram and established business connections and networking in LinkedIn. I have made friends through my mentor, and the real estate clubs and associations where I am a member, or associated with. You can strike up a conversation anywhere, at any opportunity, and establish a great contact for your own interests and benefits. Engage with other people and put yourself out there, so you can make great contacts. Make use of these friendships and connections to form rewarding relationships that can be mutually beneficial and can help you grow personally, professionally and financially.

Keep up with people
If we want to maintain a good relationship, we have to maintain contacting them. We'll fall off the radar and lose them. We can send a quick email or call them. Just check in and say hello. If these people are important to us, we should not forget to keep up with them. They may not immediately jump at the chance to help us when we reach out to them, after not talking to them for a long time.

Build trust
If we are honest and have integrity, it is easy for people to trust us. If we show dependability, reliability and even sacrifice our own interests to help someone, then we earn the trust of others. Try to do things right for others and it will come back to you.

Remember people on important occasions
Nothing makes a person happier than to be remembered on his/her birthday, and important dates and events in one's life. We can send gifts, flowers, notes, cards, greetings, emails, letters, text messages or meet them in person to say our

greetings. We can treat them to lunch or dinner, or a show or an event. This pays off in the long run towards our success and happiness.

Accept people the way they are
We are all different and at different stages of growth with different family background and cultures. Avoid judging. We do not have to agree with them in order to form a relationship with them.

Forgive
I have learned a good lesson to forgive everyone who has hurt me or caused me pain. Everyone - a partner in marriage, a friend, a relative, even myself. This frees me from grudges and bitterness. Forgiveness will lead you to move on to the other positive parts of your life. It gives us peace, understanding, and empathy and compassion for the one who hurt you. Letting go of grudges and bitterness brings us to greater spiritual and psychological well-being, and higher self-esteem. When you forgive someone, it releases the anger, thoughts of revenge and the wound in your heart and mind.

A great lesson for me all these years about relationships is to put "me, me, me" last, build better relationships with everyone through positivity, and to listen to other people, and to let go of the temptation to judge.

For what does it profit the world if I lose the important relationships with people that I care?

Be a good person and all good follows...

ACKNOWLEDGEMENTS

I would like to thank **Raymond Aaron** for the education, wisdom and guidance on how to write a book, successfully and efficiently, in two weeks' time.

I would like to thank my Personal Book Architect, **Christina Clarke**, who thought my goal to launch this book for April 2016 "Create Your Own Economy" was very ambitious. She answered my questions and guided me patiently to get this done on time.

Kudos to my Editor, **Lisa Browning,** who did a great job in editing this book. Thank you for seeing all the grammatical errors and making the corrections that made this book really look good and a lot better to read.

I would like to thank my four children **Laura, Rose, JR** and **Dino** for being there for me in my happiness and challenges; for supporting me when I was writing this book.

I would like to thank the father of my four children, **Engr. Fidelino Tinapay**, for his wisdom and for introducing me to the world of real estate. This changed my life and is continuously giving me success and a brand new world.

I would like to thank my mentor, **Sunil Tulsiani**. He taught me how to set bigger goals and fearlessly buy real estate in the USA. He taught me how to be a coach and motivated me to write a book and now bringing me to the next level of real estate investing.

I would like to thank **Caldic Canada, Inc.**'s management and staff for the work-life experiences, challenges, associations and friendships.

I would like to thank **Keller Williams Real Estate, Associates, Brokerage** for the best real estate trainings I have gained – BOLD, Ignite, Family Reunion among so many. I am proud to be a part of the great culture and company that is Keller Williams!

I want to thank **Union Carbide Philippines Inc,** now Energizer, my first employer that molded me into what I am today, that taught me that success and happiness is just a by- product of good habits and that true friendships are a lifetime and a treasure

ABOUT THE AUTHOR

Cora Cristobal is a real estate investor, realtor, coach and author with over 20 years of real estate experience. She has owned two (2) real estate brokerages in the Philippines – Cristin Realty and TC Realty & Development Corp. Her real estate investment experience and portfolio covers Canada, USA and the Philippines.

A Certified Public Accountant by profession, Cora quit her manufacturing office manager job in an American multinational company where she worked for over 11 years so that she can focus on her family. She decided to get a license as a real estate broker, so she can work on her own time. This is one of the best decisions she has made in her life as this allowed her to spend more time to taking care of the family, and maximized her money making potential as she concentrated in real estate investing.

She started by buying a piece of a subdivision lot where she lived, and sold it at four times the price, after a few months. That experience motivated her to continue buying and selling real estate at the same time that she was helping other people also buy and sell real estate. In the famous *"Fairways and Bluewater"* project in Boracay, Philippines, she became the Number 1 Area Sales Director for selling 52 shares in one month.

She is presently focusing on investing in USA, as she is taking advantage of the opportunity of lower prices. Her strategy is to buy, in joint ventures with other like-minded investors, lower than market value properties that need rehab and repairs, get a tenant and wait until the prices bounce back up. She firmly believes that the opportunity is greener on the other side of the fence as real estate prices in Canada have become more challenging to investors. She is now a coach and an author and continues to help buyers and investors in both Canada and the USA.

For those who want to contact Cora, she may be reached at cora.cristobal@gmail.com.